Analysing UNSEEN TEXTS

For English Standard & English Advanced

Student Workbook for Section I, Paper 1

First published in 2023, reprinted in 2024.

Insight Publications Pty Ltd
3/350 Charman Road
Cheltenham Victoria 3192
Australia

Tel: +61 3 8571 4950
Fax: +61 3 8571 0257
Email: books@insightpublications.com.au

www.insightpublications.com.au

A catalogue record for this book is available from the National Library of Australia

Analysing Unseen Texts: For English Standard & English Advanced
Amanda Lee

ISBN:

9781923016262

Edited by Lisa Neale
Proofread by Fiona Wallace
Cover by Melisa Paredes
Internal design by Ana Maria Sastre
Printed by Markono Print Media Pte Ltd

Contents

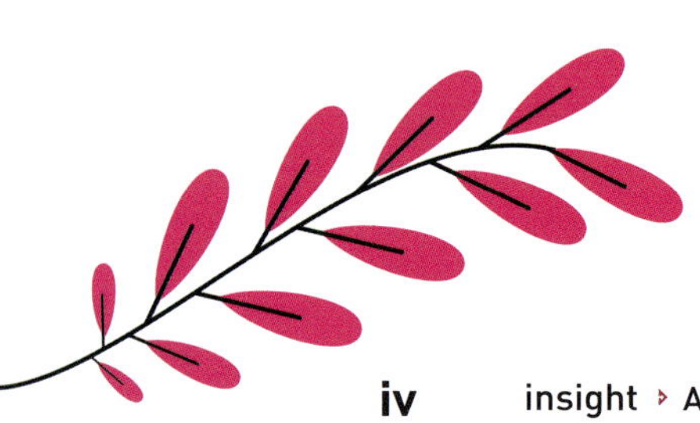

1 CHAPTER What to expect in Section I

In this chapter you will cover:

- the Common Module: Texts and Human Experiences
- responding to unseen texts
- strategies and tips for the examination.

The Common Module: Texts and Human Experiences

In the HSC English examinations, all English Standard and English Advanced students complete both Section I and Section II of Paper 1.

Section I is based upon the Common Module: Texts and Human Experiences. While there are separate Standard and Advanced examination papers, some questions and/or unseen texts may be shared across both papers, such as this question which appeared in both the Standard and Advanced papers in the 2022 HSC examination:

In what ways does Azzam celebrate togetherness?

- English Advanced Question 1 (3 marks) Text 1 – Poem
- English Standard Question 3 (3 marks) Text 3 – Poem

Some questions and texts will only appear in either the Standard examination or the Advanced examination. This ensures that there are:

- a variety of moderated questions across the papers
- questions at a level of difficulty suitable for English Standard students
- questions at a level of difficulty suitable for English Advanced students
- some shared questions that are at a suitable level for both English Standard and English Advanced students.

The questions in Section I are worth a total of 20 marks, ranging from 2 marks for a question to 8 marks for a question. In the last three years, 3, 4, and 5 mark questions have tended to be the most common.

Many questions may ask you to respond to only one unseen text at a time, but you may also be asked to write a comparison between two or more of the unseen texts, which requires a more structured response. The number of questions and the mark values for each question will vary from year to year.

The only constant for Section I is that it will be worth 20 marks. To help you understand this, here are the mark values for the last three years of the HSC English examination, Section I, Paper 1:

Paper	Number of questions	Mark allocation	Total marks
2022 English Advanced examination:	5	3 marks + 4 marks + 4 marks + 3 marks + 6 marks	20 marks
2022 English Standard examination:	5	4 marks + 5 marks + 3 marks + 4 marks + 4 marks	20 marks
2021 English Advanced examination:	5	3 marks + 3 marks + 4 marks + 4 marks + 6 marks	20 marks
2021 English Standard examination:	5	4 marks + 6 marks + 3 marks + 3 marks + 4 marks	20 marks
2020 English Advanced examination:	4	5 marks + 5 marks + 4 marks + 6 marks	20 marks
2020 English Standard examination:	4	4 marks + 6 marks + 5 marks + 5 marks	20 marks

Responding to unseen texts

There are usually between 4 and 6 unseen texts which can include **fiction** (e.g. novel extracts, short stories), **nonfiction** (e.g. biography, memoir, speeches), **poetry** (e.g. poetry extracts or complete poems), **visual texts** (e.g. art works, comics, graphic novels, picture books, photographs, screenshots from films) and **multimodal/digital** (e.g. online articles, websites, blogs, interviews).

These unseen texts are often captioned with the text type, author and occasionally publication details which can help you to discern the context and purpose of the text. Unfamiliar words are often marked with an asterisk and defined at the bottom of the page. Ensure that you take note of these details to help support your understanding of the meaning of the text.

Students often find Section I of the examination rather challenging. It is more skills-based than the other parts of the English examinations which you can better prepare for by studying known content. However, you can prepare for this section of the examination, too. You will know the conceptual basis of this unit due to your study of the Common Module: Texts and Human Experiences, and you can build your knowledge of textual features and techniques, and develop your reading, comprehension and analysis strategies.

All questions in Section I are based on the key terms and concepts from the Common Module: Texts and Human Experiences Syllabus rubric. You will need to be familiar with what each of these key terms means.

Use this rubric as a guide for:

- **WHAT you need to be identifying in the text (what is the central human experience in this text?)**
- **HOW this idea is conveyed to the audience (what language features and techniques are used in the text?)**
- **WHY this is significant (what does the audience think, feel, or realise about the human experience as a result of reading this text?)**

When reviewing your practice responses to short answer questions, you should always be able to identify where you have addressed the what, how and why. This is a good basic checklist to help you assess whether you have answered the question well.

There are several acronyms being used to teach analytical writing. Some of the most popular include:

TEEL or PEEL

Topic sentence or Point + **Evidence (technique and quote)** + **Elaboration** + **Link**

WHAT **HOW** **WHY**

PETA

Point + **Example** + **Technique** + **Analysis**

WHAT **HOW** **WHY**

QTEA

Question + **Technique** + **Example** + **Analysis**

WHAT **HOW** **WHY**

A reliable approach to prepare for Section I of the examination is to routinely complete practice questions so you are refining your ability to respond to a wide variety of short texts. You may, for example, be unfamiliar with visual or multimodal analysis if you have not studied it recently. You should use this workbook to supplement your study and ensure that you can recall the common techniques that are found in the various types of texts. You should be completing practice questions throughout your Year 12 course, ideally every week or fortnight. Considering the relatively manageable length of unseen texts and expected responses to the questions, it is feasible for you to include this practice in your regular study schedule. Practice is the best way to boost your responding and writing skills.

Strategies and tips for the examination

Paper 1 of the HSC English examination has the following format:

- Reading time – 10 minutes (no writing is allowed during this time)
- Working time – 1 hour and 30 minutes
    - Section I – short answer questions about unseen texts (20 marks)
    - Section II – sustained response about your prescribed text (20 marks).

All questions in Paper 1 focus on the Common Module: Texts and Human Experiences. The following eight tips have been created to help you prepare effectively for Paper 1. It may be worth going back to these tips once you are ready to tackle practice questions and of course before the examination.

Tip #1 **You should complete Section I before completing Section II.**

WHY? You should make the most of your reading time and complete the short answer questions while the texts you have just read are still fresh in your mind. If you complete your Section II response first, you will waste time having to re-read all of the short texts when you return to complete Section I. Remember that the two sections are of equal value, each allocated 20 marks.

Tip #2 **Read each question carefully to identify exactly what it is asking you to do.**

WHY? This will determine how much detail you need to go into. The imperative verb in the question is a good indicator of this. The most common imperative verbs and their definitions are listed in the table opposite.

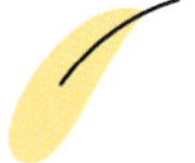

VERB	DEFINITION
Identify	Recognise and name
Analyse	Identify components and the relationship between them; draw out and relate implications
Compare	Show how things are similar or different
Contrast	Show how things are different or opposite
Describe	Provide characteristics and features
Explain	Relate cause and effect; make the relationships between things evident; provide why and/or how
Evaluate	Make a judgement based on criteria; determine the value of
Critically (analyse/evaluate)	Add a degree or level of accuracy, depth, knowledge and understanding, logic, questioning, reflection and quality to (analyse/ evaluate)

Tip #3 **Read the questions and identify what is being asked *before* reading the unseen texts.**

WHY? Once reading time begins, go straight to the questions and then read the corresponding short text. This will ensure that you are looking for the specific concepts and language techniques required to address each question accurately. Some students take note of EVERYTHING they notice about a text which is often not necessary in this section. If you know, for example, that the question is specifically asking how imagery is used to convey happiness, you will be able to find examples of imagery conveying happiness as you read that text.

Tip #4 **Write responses whose length is proportionate to the allocated mark values.**

WHY? A common mistake in this section is overwriting the responses to the first few questions in a manner that is disproportionate to the mark allocation. If a question is worth 3 marks, you should not be writing over a page in response to it. Write what you need to get the marks and move on to the other questions. Many students don't attempt the last question/s because they have run out of time. Others write the same amount for a 3 mark question as they do for a 5 mark comparative question. You need to be mindful of this during the examination so that you are making the most of your words and your time. In the HSC examination, writing booklets include a number of lines provided for your answer, as an indication of how much you should be writing. In recent examinations, some additional lines have also been provided with the instruction to use them if necessary: for example, 'If you need additional space to answer Question 3 use the lines below'. Use these as guidance to keep yourself on track.

Tip #5 **Make sure you are managing your time.**

WHY? While this is an important skill for every section, it is especially important for Section I. Assuming that you have split your time evenly between Section I and Section II, you have 45 minutes to write responses worth 20 marks. This works out to roughly 2.25 minutes per mark. Some students find it helpful to write time limits for each question. For example:

- 3 marks = approximately 6 mins
- 5 marks = approximately 11 mins
- 7 marks = approximately 16 mins

Time management for this part of the examination paper is best achieved through routine practising of these questions under the allocated time limits.

Tip #6 **Re-read your topic sentence to make sure you have answered the question.**

WHY? To avoid just writing a list of techniques that does not prove that you comprehend the text, take the extra few seconds to re-read your topic sentence and ensure you have **identified** what each of the key terms refer to in the text. Look at the following sample sentences in response to this question:

Analyse how the poem conveys a shared human experience. (4 marks)

> ***Sentence 1:*** *The metaphor of 'leaving the nest and flying free' is used to represent how the persona feels when leaving home.*

This example has launched immediately into analysis but now it has no focus. This is a very common mistake that students make because, in the panic of the examination, it is easy to default to analysing every technique they can find during the reading time. This sentence has ignored the 'shared human experience' part of the question and has not identified what that shared human experience is.

> ***Sentence 2:*** *The poem uses metaphor and alliteration to convey a shared human experience.*

This example is a little better than the first, as it is clearer that this student is trying to answer the question. However, the student has only repeated the key term from the question; they have not demonstrated that they actually know what the shared human experience is. If the student elaborated on this shared experience in the rest of their response, they could still write their way up into getting 4 marks, but if they did not make this clear, this response would be limited to the 2–3 range, even if the language techniques were accurately identified and analysed.

> ***Sentence 3:*** *The poem uses metaphor and alliteration to convey how the persona connected with their father over their shared experience of leaving home, which is a common human challenge.*

This sentence makes it clear that **the student knows what the shared experience is**. The specificity of the response also indicates that the student has comprehended the meaning of the poem, which is essential for gaining full marks. Set yourself up for success by making sure the topic sentence has this level of clarity.

Tip #7 In a comparative question, structure the response as a mini-essay.

WHY? Comparative questions imply that you need to analyse the similarities and/or differences between two texts. If you write all your analysis in a single paragraph, it can be difficult to discern what you think the similarities and/or differences are. This comparative type of question is normally found in the final question. Any comparative analysis of how two texts explore a concept, whether focused on differences or similarities, needs to include the composers language features as an integrated part of showing your understanding of how the meaning is constructed.

Two basic structures for a mini-essay are included below:

Structure One

- **Mini-thesis** – Answer the question, identify the texts and specify what the human experience is in both of the texts.
- **Body paragraph 1** – Identify what the human experience is in Text 1 and follow up with textual evidence to support your assertion.
- **Body paragraph 2** – Identify what the human experience is in Text 2 and follow up with textual evidence to support your assertion.
- **Conclusion** – Write one to two sentences reinforcing your mini-thesis.

Structure Two

- **Mini-thesis** – Answer the question, identify the texts and specify what the human experience is in both of the texts.
- **Body paragraph 1** – Identify the similarities between Text 1 and Text 2 then support with evidence such as the language/techniques (depending on the text form) from both texts.
- **Body paragraph 2** – Identify the differences between Text 1 and Text 2 then support with evidence from both texts.
- **Conclusion** – Write one to two sentences reinforcing your mini-thesis.

The structure you choose will depend on the question's mark value and the imperative verb/s.

Use words in your response that show you are *analysing*, not simply *describing*.

WHY? Very often you are being marked on your ability to *analyse* the text, rather than *describe* the text. Examine the following table to understand the difference between these two verbs. When you are *describing*, you only need to name and identify the object of the description and then identify some features and characteristics.

When you are *analysing*, you must name and identify what you are analysing, identify some features/characteristics, write about the effect of these characteristics and connect your discussion of relevant examples to the question you have been asked.

DESCRIBE	ANALYSE
Features and characteristics	Features and characteristics
Name and Identify	Name and Identify
	Write about the effect of the characteristics
	Connect to example
	Look at the relationships between different features and characteristics (for more complex questions or comparative responses).

Refer to this information when completing the sample responses in Chapter 7. A useful self-review activity is to highlight each analytical word that you have used in your response to ensure that you have analysed your text instead of just describing it.

See Chapter 7 for a list of useful words to use in analytical responses.

2 CHAPTER

Strategies and techniques for analysing fiction

In this chapter you will cover:

- points to consider when analysing fiction
- common fiction features and techniques
- fiction texts: guided note-taking and practice questions.

Points to consider when analysing fiction

Examples of fiction include short stories, vignettes, drabbles, microfiction, novels and novellas.

Fiction relies on a fusion of plot, character and setting, constructed by the author to convey particular themes and ideas. It is designed to engage the reader through emotions, ensuring that there is connection between the reader and the experiences/characters within the text.

This connection may be created through moments of shared realisation and empathy. For example, the reader is guided to feel recognition of what is depicted and identify with an emotion or empathise with a character's reaction or behaviour. However, connection may also be created through involving the reader in new experiences or insights. For example, the reader has no personal experience with what is being depicted, but can connect to this new experience, place or character due to the skill with which it has been depicted; the author can make the reader 'feel' like they've had a new experience by reading the fictional text.

Given the length and timing of the examination, you will probably be reading extracts from a novel or story rather than a complete narrative. This means you will need to discern the prevalent ideas in the sections you have been given.

Here are some questions to guide your thought process when analysing fiction:

1. What is happening within the text?

It is *vital* to understand the basics of the narrative within the text. You need to prove that you have *comprehended* the text, so you must figure out what is happening first to ensure that your answer reflects that comprehension. Not all of the following options will be present within every fiction extract, but you should aim to identify as many as possible. A technique-driven response that analyses language use but shows minimal understanding of what is happening in the text will make it very difficult to access high marks. Therefore, make sure you try to answer at least some of the following questions:

- **Who is the character/s?** How old are they, and what are their relationships like with themselves, others and the world around them? Can you tell their occupation or attitude? What adjectives would you use to describe them and why?
- **What is happening to the character/what is the character doing and why?** What is the reaction of your character to the action/events around them? What does that tell you about the character and their motivations/perspective on the world and on human experiences?
- **Where/when is the story set, and is that important?** How does the setting and timing affect the narrative? Is the setting symbolic in some way? Is the narrative set within a particular historical period that affects meaning?

2. What is the implicit meaning within the text and how is this conveyed using character/plot/setting?

What human experiences are being represented in the text? This is a very broad question; however, it is extremely important that you go beyond the literal action of the story and connect this to the themes or messages that the author is conveying about human experiences. Some common human experiences in fiction texts include:

- Different cultural experiences
- Knowledge of the self and the importance of identity
- Important moments in life like graduating, finding a new job, becoming a parent, etc.
- The importance of art and creativity in the human experience
- The importance of celebrating/acknowledging the past
- Spiritual, emotional, psychological, physical and intellectual growth
- Relationships.

3. What language/structural features are used by the author to accentuate features of the character/plot/setting?

How is the author conveying and emphasising the text's ideas? Consider:

- Figurative language: for example, sensory language/imagery, metaphor, simile, emotive language, symbolism and pathetic fallacy.
- Characterisation: features of the character that build up a clear impression of their personality, motivations and behaviour
- Structure: for example, syntax and narrative features such as:
    - Repetition of key ideas, words or lines
    - Truncated or run-on sentences, punctuated in a manner that creates a sense of rhythm/pace to the narrative
    - Use of dialogue/internal monologue and the modality of this feature
    - Narrative perspective: first, second, third, omnipresent, etc.
    - Structural features particular to the opening and/or ending of a narrative – this relates to fiction extracts which are clearly introducing/beginning a narrative or ending it (some extracts will be taken from the middle of a story).

4. What other significant features or techniques do you notice?

There are other fiction features and techniques (which are listed in the table below), but those mentioned in the three questions above will be the most common language forms and features that you will readily identify in most fiction texts. You should look for these aspects first before examining other significant features.

Common fiction features and techniques

FIGURATIVE LANGUAGE TECHNIQUES	
Simile	An explicit comparison between two things through the use of connecting words, usually 'like' or 'as'.
Metaphor	A comparison of two subjects without the use of 'like' or 'as', instead asserting that one thing is the other, or is a substitute for the other.
Imagery or sensory language	Language that appeals to the senses, helping the reader to imagine specific sensations which evoke an emotional and/or intellectual response: • visual imagery (sight) • kinaesthetic/tactile imagery (touch) • olfactory imagery (smell) • auditory imagery (sound) • gustatory imagery (taste).

Synaesthesia

A figure of speech in which one sense is described using terms from another. Examples of synaesthesia are often in the form of a simile or metaphor, as this is an easy way to link two otherwise unconnected images. For example, 'the bright sound of a siren' fuses visual and auditory words together.

Symbolism

Giving objects a certain meaning that is different from their literal meaning. Writers use symbolism to tie certain things that may initially seem unimportant to more universal themes. The symbols then represent these grander ideas or qualities.

Motif

An idea or symbolically significant object or event that is repeated throughout a work of literature. Motifs may come in the form of recurring imagery, language, structure or contrasts. The development of motifs in a work of literature often contributes to mood and/or theme.

Allusion

A brief and indirect reference to a person, place, thing or idea of historical, cultural, literary or political significance. It does not describe in detail the person or thing to which it refers. It is just a passing reference and the writer expects the reader to possess enough knowledge to observe the allusion and grasp its importance and meaning in a text. When the reference is to a specific literary work, this can also be called intertextuality.

Juxtaposition

Placing two unlike things next to one another to prompt the reader to reflect on their similarities and differences.

Personification

A figure of speech in which a non-living or inanimate thing is given living, often human, attributes. The non-living object is often portrayed in such a way that we feel it can act like a human being. For example, when we say, 'The sky weeps', we are giving the sky the ability to cry, which is a human quality.

Hyperbole

Derived from a Greek word meaning 'over-casting'. A figure of speech that involves an exaggeration of ideas for the sake of emphasis.

Pun or paronomasia

A play on words that produces a humorous effect by using a word that suggests two or more meanings, or by exploiting similar sounding words that have different meanings.

Synecdoche

A figure of speech in which a word or phrase that refers to a part of something is substituted to stand in for the whole, or vice versa. For example, the phrase 'all hands on deck' is a demand for all of the crew to help, yet the word 'hands' – just a part of the crew – stands in for the whole crew.

Paradox

A statement that appears to be self-contradictory or silly, but which may include a latent truth. It is also used to illustrate an opinion or statement contrary to accepted traditional ideas. A paradox is often used to make a reader think over an idea in an innovative way.

Pathetic fallacy

Describing nature or inanimate things in a way that is sympathetic to, reflective of or prophetic about the events in the plot and/or the emotions of the characters.

AURAL FEATURES

Consonance

A literary device in which a consonant sound is repeated in words that are in close proximity. The repeated sound can appear anywhere in the words, unlike in alliteration where the repeated consonant sound must occur in the stressed part of the word.

Sibilance

A special kind of consonance in which the repeated consonant sound is s, sh, z or any other sibilant sound. Sibilance occurs when the repetition of these specific consonants are in words in close proximity to each other.

Alliteration

The repetition of consonant sounds, generally at the beginning of words or the stressed parts of words in close proximity to each other.

Assonance

The repetition of vowel sounds in words in close proximity to each other.

Onomatopoeia

Words that imitate a sound effect. These words mimic the things they are describing.

OTHER NARRATIVE FEATURES

Emotive language

Language that elicits an emotional response in the reader.

High modality language

Language that conveys a high degree of certainty through the manner in which it's expressed.

Diction/lexical choice

The selection of a word for its particular meaning, implication or connotation. The words and style of expression that an author uses in a work of literature can have a significant effect on the tone of the text and on how readers perceive the characters.

Lexical chain

The use of a chain of words within a short segment of text which work together to cumulate meaning. For example, within a paragraph an author could use the words 'stab', 'blood' and 'screaming' which, when combined in the reader's mind, give a greater impression of violence than just one of these words would create.

Repetition

Repeating the same words or phrases a few times to make an idea clearer and more memorable.

Tone

The emotion or attitude with which something is said or written. How is the character/author feeling as they express themselves? Use adjectives to describe tone, such as 'reflective', 'regretful', 'nostalgic', 'wistful' or 'pensive'.

Mood

The emotion created by the text within the audience/reader. Mood can also be referred to as the 'atmosphere' of a text. Certain feelings are evoked in readers through words and descriptions. Mood can be developed in a text through various methods, including setting descriptions, tone and diction.

Character type

Character foil, protagonist, antagonist, 'everyman' character, etc. You could look up 'trope' or 'archetype' for a more detailed understanding; however, you won't often need this to respond to short-answer questions.

Flashback

When a character remembers an earlier event that happened before the current point of the story. There are two types of flashbacks – those that recount events that happened before the story started ('external analepsis') and those that take the reader back to an event that already happened but that the character is considering again ('internal analepsis'). Stories that have flashbacks are referred to as non-linear since the events are not being told in chronological order.

Microcosm

A community, place, or situation regarded as encapsulating in miniature the characteristics of something much larger.

Narrative perspective/ form

First person
e.g. 'I went down the stairs.'

Second person
e.g. 'you went down the stairs.'

Third person
e.g. 'John went down the stairs.'

Omnipresent narrator
third person, third person limited, etc. – when the narrator can be 'present' in multiple places and times at once.

Omniscient narrator
when the narrator can 'see all', be everywhere and know the thoughts of all characters.

Unreliable narrator
when the narrative perspective is constructed with enough clues for the reader to realise that the narrator cannot be trusted – the narrator's view is limited by their lack of knowledge and/or personal perspective/bias.

Stream of consciousness
a narrative form where the author writes in a way that mimics or parallels a character's internal thoughts. Sometimes this device is also called 'internal monologue', and often the style of language incorporates the natural chaos of thoughts and feelings that occur in any of our minds at any given time. This still has to be punctuated sufficiently correctly to allow the reader to follow the character's thoughts.

Fiction texts: guided note-taking and practice questions

Use the note-taking questions below to guide your thinking about each fiction extract, then answer the practice examination questions that follow.

Fiction extract 1

Novel extract from *The Great Gatsby* by F Scott Fitzgerald

Then wear the gold hat, if that will move her;
If you can bounce high, bounce for her too,
Till she cry 'Lover, gold-hatted, high-bouncing lover,
I must have you!'

Thomas Parke D'Invilliers

In my younger and more vulnerable years my father gave me some advice that I've been turning over in my mind ever since.

'Whenever you feel like criticizing anyone,' he told me, 'just remember that all the people in this world haven't had the advantages that you've had.'

He didn't say any more, but we've always been unusually communicative in a reserved way, and I understood that he meant a great deal more than that. In consequence, I'm inclined to reserve all judgements, a habit that has opened up many curious natures to me and also made me the victim of not a few veteran bores. The abnormal mind is quick to detect and attach itself to this quality when it appears in a normal person, and so it came about that in college I was unjustly accused of being a politician, because I was privy to the secret griefs of wild, unknown men. Most of the confidences were unsought – frequently I have feigned sleep, preoccupation, or a hostile levity when I realized by some unmistakable sign that an intimate revelation was quivering on the horizon; for the intimate revelations of young men, or at least the terms in which they express them, are usually plagiaristic and marred by obvious suppressions. Reserving judgements is a matter of infinite hope. I am still a little afraid of missing something if I forget that, as my father snobbishly suggested, and I snobbishly repeat, a sense of the fundamental decencies is parcelled out unequally at birth.

And, after boasting this way of my tolerance, I come to the admission that it has a limit. Conduct may be founded on the hard rock or the wet marshes, but after a certain point I don't care what it's founded on. When I came back from the East last autumn I felt that I wanted the world to be in uniform and at a sort of moral attention forever; I wanted no more riotous excursions with privileged glimpses into the human heart. Only Gatsby, the man who gives his name to this book, was exempt from my reaction – Gatsby, who represented everything for which I have an unaffected scorn. If personality is an unbroken series of successful gestures, then there was something gorgeous about him, some heightened sensitivity to the promises of life, as if he were related to one of those intricate machines that register earthquakes ten thousand miles away. This responsiveness had nothing to do with that flabby impressionability which is dignified under the name of the 'creative temperament' – it was an extraordinary gift for hope, a romantic readiness such as I have never found in any other person and which it is not likely I shall ever find again. No – Gatsby turned out all right at the end; it is what preyed on Gatsby, what foul dust floated in the wake of his dreams that temporarily closed out my interest in the abortive sorrows and short-winded elations of men.

My family have been prominent, well-to-do people in this Middle Western city for three generations. The Carraways are something of a clan, and we have a tradition that we're descended from the Dukes of Buccleuch, but the actual founder of my line was my grandfather's brother, who came here in fifty-one, sent a substitute to the Civil War, and started the wholesale hardware business that my father carries on today.

I never saw this great-uncle, but I'm supposed to look like him – with special reference to the rather hard-boiled painting that hangs in father's office. I graduated from New Haven in 1915, just a quarter of a century after my father, and a little later I participated in that delayed Teutonic migration known as the Great War. I enjoyed the counter-raid so thoroughly that I came back restless. Instead of being the warm centre of the world, the Middle West now seemed like the ragged edge of the universe – so I decided to go East and learn the bond business. Everybody I knew was in the bond business, so I supposed it could support one more single man. All my aunts and uncles talked it over as if they were choosing a prep school for me, and finally said, 'Why – ye-es,' with very grave, hesitant faces. Father agreed to finance me for a year, and after various delays I came East, permanently, I thought, in the spring of twenty-two.

The practical thing was to find rooms in the city, but it was a warm season, and I had just left a country of wide lawns and friendly trees, so when a young man at the office suggested that we take a house together in a commuting town, it sounded like a great idea. He found the house, a weather-beaten cardboard bungalow at eighty a month, but at the last minute the firm ordered him to Washington, and I went out to the country alone. I had a dog – at least I had him for a few days until he ran away – and an old Dodge and a Finnish woman, who made my bed and cooked breakfast and muttered Finnish wisdom to herself over the electric stove.

It was lonely for a day or so until one morning some man, more recently arrived than I, stopped me on the road.

'How do you get to West Egg village?' he asked helplessly.

I told him. And as I walked on I was lonely no longer. I was a guide, a pathfinder, an original settler. He had casually conferred on me the freedom of the neighbourhood.

And so with the sunshine and the great bursts of leaves growing on the trees, just as things grow in fast movies, I had that familiar conviction that life was beginning over again with the summer.

There was so much to read, for one thing, and so much fine health to be pulled down out of the young breath-giving air. I bought a dozen volumes on banking and credit and investment securities, and they stood on my shelf in red and gold like new money from the mint, promising to unfold the shining secrets that only Midas and Morgan and Maecenas knew. And I had the high intention of reading many other books besides. I was rather literary in college – one year I wrote a series of very solemn and obvious editorials for the Yale News – and now I was going to bring back all such things into my life and become again that most limited of all specialists, the 'well-rounded man.' This isn't just an epigram – life is much more successfully looked at from a single window, after all.

Read this example of guided note-taking for Fiction extract 1.

1. What is happening within the text?
   - Who is the character/s?
   - What is happening to the character/what is the character doing and why?

   He has moved to West Egg village and is reading new books, presumably to pursue a lucrative career in bonds. He has mentioned his father, a man called Gatsby and features of his new life as he has settled in West Egg.

   - Where and when is the story set, and is that important?

   This is set in the 1920s based on the narrator graduating in 1915 and moving to West Egg in 1922. Contextually this means the story is set after WWI, in America. This could be important since this was a period of shifting worldviews.

2. What is the implicit meaning within the text and how is this conveyed using character/plot/setting?

   The tone of the narrator is slightly bitter as he does not seem to have a favourable impression of mankind and the world. The past tense in the opening compared to his more optimistic reflections upon moving imply that his experiences in West Egg have changed him.

3. What language/structural features are used by the author to accentuate features of the character/plot/setting?

   Past tense, metaphors, visual imagery and emotive language help to capture the narrator's thoughts and feelings on the world, himself, his own family and the other character, Gatsby.

4. What other significant features or techniques do you notice?

   Pathetic fallacy is used to reflect what the narrator's fresh start is supposed to provide for him – e.g. 'And so with the sunshine and the great bursts of leaves growing on the trees, just as things grow in fast movies, I had that familiar conviction that life was beginning over again with the summer.'

Sample question and response for Fiction extract 1

Explain how the fiction extract explores how introspection can lead an individual to a greater understanding of the world. (5 marks)

The narrator in Fiction extract 1 is reflecting on his own privileged upbringing and how his interactions with others have shaped his perception of men and the world. The narrator shares an anecdote about advice he was given from his father about criticising others and remembering 'that all the people in this world haven't had the advantages that you've had.' The narrator continues to reflect on how this advice influenced him to 'reserve all judgements' when he encountered new people in university. However, the narrator continues reflecting on his father's advice and concludes somewhat pessimistically that 'a sense of the fundamental decencies is parcelled out unequally at birth.' This metaphor captures the narrator's realisation that wealth and birthright have a profound effect on the success of a man and how he is perceived by others, making it impossible for the average person to reserve judgements on others and consider that they have not had the same advantages. The narrator also reflects on a person he met, Gatsby, in a tone of admiration, describing him as 'gorgeous' and having 'some heightened sensitivity to the promises of life.' Despite the narrator remembering his fresh start in life as he 'came East', this romanticised view of the world is something that the narrator lacks in the present, presumably having had his youthful optimism destroyed by his experiences in West Egg in the past. The narrator has therefore gained a more realistic but pessimistic view of the world and how a man is judged more on his 'advantages' than on the integrity of his character.

Fiction extract 2

Novel extract from *The War of the Worlds* by HG Wells

Saturday lives in my memory as a day of suspense. It was a day of lassitude too, hot and close, with, I am told, a rapidly fluctuating barometer. I had slept but little, though my wife had succeeded in sleeping, and I rose early. I went into my garden before breakfast and stood listening, but towards the common there was nothing stirring but a lark.

The milkman came as usual. I heard the rattle of his chariot and I went round to the side gate to ask the latest news. He told me that during the night the Martians had been surrounded by troops, and that guns were expected. Then – a familiar, reassuring note – I heard a train running towards Woking.

'They aren't to be killed,' said the milkman, 'if that can possibly be avoided.'

I saw my neighbour gardening, chatted with him for a time, and then strolled in to breakfast. It was a most unexceptional morning. My neighbour was of opinion that the troops would be able to capture or to destroy the Martians during the day.

'It's a pity they make themselves so unapproachable,' he said. 'It would be curious to know how they live on another planet; we might learn a thing or two.'

He came up to the fence and extended a handful of strawberries, for his gardening was as generous as it was enthusiastic. At the same time he told me of the burning of the pine woods about the Byfleet Golf Links.

'They say,' said he, 'that there's another of those blessed things fallen there – number two. But one's enough, surely. This lot'll cost the insurance people a pretty penny before everything's settled.' He laughed with an air of the greatest good humour as he said this. The woods, he said, were still burning, and pointed out a haze of smoke to me. 'They will be hot under foot for days, on account of the thick soil of pine needles and turf,' he said, and then grew serious over 'poor Ogilvy.'

After breakfast, instead of working, I decided to walk down towards the common. Under the railway bridge I found a group of soldiers – sappers, I think, men in small round caps, dirty red jackets unbuttoned, and showing their blue shirts, dark trousers, and boots coming to the calf. They told me no one was allowed over the canal, and, looking along the road towards the bridge, I saw one of the Cardigan men standing sentinel there. I talked with these soldiers for a time; I told them of my sight of the Martians on the previous evening. None of them had seen the Martians, and they had but the vaguest ideas of them, so that they plied me with questions. They said that they did not know who had authorised the movements of the troops; their idea was that a dispute had arisen at the Horse Guards. The ordinary sapper is a great deal better educated than the common soldier, and they discussed the peculiar conditions of the possible fight with some acuteness. I described the Heat-Ray to them, and they began to argue among themselves.

'Crawl up under cover and rush 'em, say I,' said one.

'Get aht!' said another. 'What's cover against this 'ere 'eat? Sticks to cook yer! What we got to do is to go as near as the ground'll let us, and then drive a trench.'

'Blow yer trenches! You always want trenches; you ought to ha' been born a rabbit Snippy.'

'Ain't they got any necks, then?' said a third, abruptly – a little, contemplative, dark man, smoking a pipe.

I repeated my description.

'Octopuses,' said he, 'that's what I calls 'em. Talk about fishers of men – fighters of fish it is this time!'

'It ain't no murder killing beasts like that,' said the first speaker.

'Why not shell the darned things strite off and finish 'em?' said the little dark man. 'You carn tell what they might do.'

'Where's your shells?' said the first speaker. 'There ain't no time. Do it in a rush, that's my tip, and do it at once.'

So they discussed it. After a while I left them, and went on to the railway station to get as many morning papers as I could.

Answer the following note-taking questions for Fiction extract 2.

1. What is happening within the text? (Who is the character, what is happening to them, where/when is this story set?)

2. What is the implicit meaning within the text and how is this conveyed using character/plot/setting?

3. What language/structural features are used by the author to accentuate features of the character/plot/setting?

4. What other significant features or techniques do you notice?

Write a response that answers the following question, using your own notes and the sample response for Fiction extract 1 as a guide.

Practice question for Fiction extract 2

Analyse how Fiction extract 2 invites the reader to reflect on the assumptions they have about war. (4 marks)

Fiction extract 3

Short story: 'The Old Things' by Jessie Anderson Chase

Like Sir Roger's neighbours peering over the hedge, I had daily observed, over my stone wall, a very old gentleman in his shirt sleeves, who pleasantly gave me the rôle of Spectator. A New-Englander of the elder type, with the heavy bent head of the thinker; but, particularly, with the piercing yet so kindly humorous blue eye that loses none of its colour with age, but seems to grow more vivid and vital with the same years that steal from the hair its hue of life and from the walnut cheek its glowing red.

Such an eye, to a lawyer like myself, accustomed to look for a human document in every human face, seemed the very epitome of eighty years: a carefree boyhood among *contemporaries* – in house furnishings, in barn and pigsty, orchard and gardens; a youth that sees already a new generation in most of these companions of his earthly pilgrimage; a middle age, forced out of the romantic sense of companionship on the road, into the persistent and finally triumphant view of using environment for ends of its own; and then old age, free to return and lavish forgotten endearments upon the 'old things!' This or the other 'landmark,' dear, and familiar from life's beginnings. These periods, all slipping unnoticed into their successors, yet each possessing a distinct and tangible outline and colour, had all had their turn at my neighbour's blue eyes. And the look that comes only at the end, when the life has been prodigal of response and of an unswerving fidelity in the storing up of values – that was the look that I valued as a thing of price.

It was a day of late summer that brought me more directly face to face with its beauty and gravity. The old gentleman appeared, in his shirt sleeves, but with plenty of ceremony in his quiet demeanour, at the door of my little 'portable' law office, at the edge of the orchard.

'I am told, sir,' he began, 'that you are an attorney at law.'

I bowed, and offered him a chair but he continued standing.

'I have come,' he said, 'to request your services in drawing up my last will and testament – that is,' he serenely emended, 'in case your vacation time is subject to such interruption.'

While I was formulating my assent he continued:

'You have no doubt, since coming into this rather communicative neighbourhood, been informed that my son owns the homestead.'

The kind, keen old eyes took on a look of what George Eliot names 'an enormous patience with the way of the world.'

'Everything belongs to John and Mary. But there are one or two little old things that they don't care about. They're up in the lean-to. The old mirror that, as a lad,

I used to see my face in over my mother's shoulder, it's still holding for me the picture of my mother smiling up at me. And the old ladder-back chair that she used to sit in and cuddle me; and switch, me, too – and maybe that took the most love of all. That's all. John and Mary don't want them. They're only old things, like myself. It's natural, perfectly natural. At their age I most probably felt just so.'

He paused and looked through the lattice, where the reddened vine-leaves were beginning to fall.

'The young leaf-buds pushing off the old leaves. It's nature.'

Before sunset – for the old man was strangely impatient – I had his 'will' signed, witnessed, and sealed. The old mirror and chair were to go to a wee, odd little old lady, called in the neighbourhood 'Miss Tabby' Titcomb because of her forty-odd cats, except for which she lived alone.

'Little Ellen,' *he* called her, as he fondly spoke of their school days together. 'Mother would have been well content if we'd hit it off together, Ellen and I. But a boy is as apt as not, when urged one way, to fly off in another; and I was at the skittish age.

'I've never said this before to any man, sir, but I'd have been a better husband to Ellen. Mary was a faithful wife, and better than I deserved. But she was not just aware, like Ellen, of where to bear on hard and where to go a little easy. That's what a man needs in a woman, sir. Ellen always knew just when and where.'

The next morning, which was Saturday, I was riding down Bare Hill Road – as it chanced, right past Miss Tabby's – when my horse shied; and that tiny old lady, with an enormous gray cat beside her, rose up from behind the lilac bushes. Bigger people than 'little Ellen' have been frightened by Prince's antics, but she quietly put her hand on his restive neck as if he were only a little larger kitten, and then spoke to me in a soft little purr of a voice:

'I've heard – and you'll excuse me – that you're a lawyer, Mr. Alden; and I've a small matter I don't wish to entrust to any one here, being private. It's a letter for Mr. Thomas Sewall, to be delivered upon my demise, which I feel is about to take place.' She spoke with a little note of relief, as if from some long strain.

I took the small envelope.

'It's just the cats,' she was moved to confide further; 'the little ones and the smart ones will all find friends. But the two *old ones*! Mr. Sewall has a notion for the old things. And' – here she hesitated long, while I breathlessly assured her of my best care for the letter – 'there's – somewhat in the note *besides* the cats,' she brought out bravely. 'You'll make sure it doesn't fall into John and Mary's hands?'

This was Saturday morning. Sunday, as I listened absent-mindedly to the slow toll of the meeting-house bell, my housekeeper remarked, on bringing in my coffee:

'Did you notice, sir? It was eighty-six. There's an old man and an old woman, both just the same age, in the village, died in the night.'

The old chair, upon which – when they were young together – the little Tom had been spanked and comforted; and the mirror, still treasuring the picture of the round, saucy phiz over his mother's shoulder, were offered at auction and bid in for a trifle by me. I would have paid gold sovereigns for them, but not into the hands of John and Mary! The cats, likewise, sit by the hearth, on which was burned to ashes the letter 'not *entirely*' about their disposal.

And the 'Old Things' that cherished these earthly companions? The minister – himself a rare 'old thing' – preached a funeral sermon for the two so strangely united by death; and his thin voice, like the tone of an old, cracked violin, still haunts me:

'Their youth is renewed like the eagle's ... And they shall run and not be weary, they shall walk and not faint.'

Answer the following note-taking questions for Fiction extract 3.

1.What is happening within the text? (Who is the character, what is happening to them, where/when is this story set?)

____

____

2.What is the implicit meaning within the text and how is this conveyed using character/plot/setting?

____

____

3. What language/structural features are used by the author to accentuate features of the character/plot/setting?

____

____

4. What other significant features or techniques do you notice?

____

____

Write a response that answers the following question, using your own notes and the sample response for Fiction extract 1 as a guide.

Practice question for Fiction extract 3

Explain how the fiction extract invites the reader to reflect on the value of connection and relationships. (4 marks)

Fiction extract 4

Novel extract from *My Brilliant Career* by Miles Franklin

'Boo, hoo! Ow, ow; Oh! oh! Me'll die. Boo, hoo. The pain, the pain! Boo, hoo!'

'Come, come, now. Daddy's little mate isn't going to turn Turk like that, is she? I'll put some fat out of the dinner-bag on it, and tie it up in my hanky. Don't cry any more now. Hush, you must not cry! You'll make old Dart buck if you kick up a row like that.'

That is my first recollection of life. I was barely three. I can remember the majestic gum-trees surrounding us, the sun glinting on their straight white trunks, and falling on the gurgling fern-banked stream, which disappeared beneath a steep scrubby hill on our left. It was an hour past noon on a long clear summer day. We were on a distant part of the run, where my father had come to deposit salt. He had left home early in the dewy morning, carrying me in front of him on a little brown pillow which my mother had made for the purpose. We had put the lumps of rock-salt in the troughs on the other side of the creek. The stringybark roof of the salt-shed which protected the troughs from rain peeped out picturesquely from the musk and peppercorn shrubs by which it was densely surrounded, and was visible from where we lunched. I refilled the quart-pot in which we had boiled our tea with water from the creek, father doused our fire out with it, and then tied the quart to the D of his saddle with a piece of green hide. The green-hide bags in which the salt had been carried were hanging on the hooks of the pack-saddle which encumbered the bay pack-horse. Father's saddle and the brown pillow were on Dart, the big grey horse on which he generally carried me, and we were on the point of making tracks for home.

Preparatory to starting, father was muzzling the dogs which had just finished what lunch we had left. This process, to which the dogs strongly objected, was rendered necessary by a cogent reason. Father had brought his strychnine flask with him that day, and in hopes of causing the death of a few dingoes, had put strong doses of its contents in several dead beasts which we had come across.

Whilst the dogs were being muzzled, I busied myself in plucking ferns and flowers. This disturbed a big black snake which was curled at the butt of a tree fern.

'Bitey! bitey!' I yelled, and father came to my rescue, despatching the reptile with his stock-whip. He had been smoking, and dropped his pipe on the ferns. I picked it up, and the glowing embers which fell from it burnt my dirty little fat fists. Hence the noise with which my story commences.

In all probability it was the burning of my fingers which so indelibly impressed the incident on my infantile mind. My father was accustomed to take me with him, but that is the only jaunt at that date which I remember, and that is all I remember of it. We were twelve miles from home, but how we reached there I do not know.

...

My mother remonstrated, opined I would be a great unwomanly tomboy. My father poohed the idea.

'Let her alone, Lucy,' he said, 'let her alone. The rubbishing conventionalities which are the curse of her sex will bother her soon enough. Let her alone!'

So, smiling and saying, 'She should have been a boy,' my mother let me alone, and I rode, and in comparison to my size made as much noise with my stock-whip as any one. Accidents had no power over me, I came unscathed out of droves of them.

Fear I knew not. Did a drunken tramp happen to kick up a row, I was always the first to confront him, and, from my majestic and roly-poly height of two feet six inches, demand what he wanted.

...

My brothers and sisters contracted mumps, measles, scarlatina, and whooping-cough. I rolled in the bed with them yet came off scot-free. I romped with dogs, climbed trees after birds' nests, drove the bullocks in the dray, under the instructions of Ben, our bullocky, and always accompanied my father when he went swimming in the clear, mountain, shrub-lined stream which ran deep and lone among the weird gullies, thickly carpeted with maidenhair and numberless other species of ferns.

My mother shook her head over me and trembled for my future, but father seemed to consider me nothing unusual. He was my hero, confidant, encyclopedia, mate, and even my religion till I was ten. Since then I have been religionless.

Richard Melvyn, you were a fine fellow in those days! A kind and indulgent parent, a chivalrous husband, a capital host, a man full of ambition and gentlemanliness.

Answer the following questions for Fiction extract 4.

1. What is happening within the text? (Who is the character, what is happening to them, where/when is this story set?)

2. What is the implicit meaning within the text and how is this conveyed using character/plot/setting?

3. What language/structural features are used by the author to accentuate features of the character/plot/setting?

4. What other significant features or techniques do you notice?

Write a response that answers the following question, using your own notes and the sample response for Fiction extract 1 as a guide.

Practice question for Fiction extract 4

How does the author invite the reader to engage with the protagonist's experience of childhood? (3 marks)

Fiction extract 5

Short story extract from '2BR02B' by Kurt Vonnegut

Everything was perfectly swell.

There were no prisons, no slums, no insane asylums, no cripples, no poverty, no wars.

All diseases were conquered. So was old age.

Death, barring accidents, was an adventure for volunteers.

The population of the United States was stabilized at forty-million souls.

One bright morning in the Chicago Lying-in Hospital, a man named Edward K. Wehling, Jr., waited for his wife to give birth. He was the only man waiting. Not many people were born a day any more.

Wehling was fifty-six, a mere stripling in a population whose average age was one hundred and twenty-nine.

X-rays had revealed that his wife was going to have triplets. The children would be his first.

Young Wehling was hunched in his chair, his head in his hand. He was so rumpled, so still and colorless as to be virtually invisible. His camouflage was perfect, since the waiting room had a disorderly and demoralized air, too. Chairs and ashtrays had been moved away from the walls. The floor was paved with spattered dropcloths.

The room was being redecorated. It was being redecorated as a memorial to a man who had volunteered to die.

A sardonic old man, about two hundred years old, sat on a stepladder, painting a mural he did not like. Back in the days when people aged visibly, his age would have been guessed at thirty-five or so. Aging had touched him that much before the cure for aging was found.

The mural he was working on depicted a very neat garden. Men and women in white, doctors and nurses, turned the soil, planted seedlings, sprayed bugs, spread fertilizer.

Men and women in purple uniforms pulled up weeds, cut down plants that were old and sickly, raked leaves, carried refuse to trash-burners.

Never, never, never – not even in medieval Holland nor old Japan – had a garden been more formal, been better tended. Every plant had all the loam, light, water, air and nourishment it could use.

A hospital orderly came down the corridor, singing under his breath a popular song:

If you don't like my kisses, honey,
Here's what I will do:
I'll go see a girl in purple,
Kiss this sad world toodle-oo.
If you don't want my lovin',
Why should I take up all this space?
I'll get off this old planet,
Let some sweet baby have my place.

The orderly looked in at the mural and the muralist. 'Looks so real,' he said, 'I can practically imagine I'm standing in the middle of it.'

'What makes you think you're not in it?' said the painter. He gave a satiric smile. 'It's called 'The Happy Garden of Life,' you know.'

'That's good of Dr. Hitz,' said the orderly.

He was referring to one of the male figures in white, whose head was a portrait of Dr. Benjamin Hitz, the hospital's Chief Obstetrician. Hitz was a blindingly handsome man.

'Lot of faces still to fill in,' said the orderly. He meant that the faces of many of the figures in the mural were still blank. All blanks were to be filled with portraits of important people on either the hospital staff or from the Chicago Office of the Federal Bureau of Termination.

'Must be nice to be able to make pictures that look like something,' said the orderly.

The painter's face curdled with scorn. 'You think I'm proud of this daub?' he said. 'You think this is my idea of what life really looks like?'

'What's your idea of what life looks like?' said the orderly.

The painter gestured at a foul drop cloth. 'There's a good picture of it,' he said. 'Frame that, and you'll have a picture a damn sight more honest than this one.'

'You're a gloomy old duck, aren't you?' said the orderly.

'Is that a crime?' said the painter.

The orderly shrugged. 'If you don't like it here, Grandpa –' he said, and he finished the thought with the trick telephone number that people who didn't want to live any more were supposed to call. The zero in the telephone number he pronounced 'naught.'

The number was: '2 B R 0 2 B.'

It was the telephone number of an institution whose fanciful sobriquets included: 'Automat,' 'Birdland,' 'Cannery,' 'Catbox,' 'De-louser,' 'Easy-go,' 'Good-by, Mother,' 'Happy Hooligan,' 'Kiss-me-quick,' 'Lucky Pierre,' 'Sheepdip,' 'Waring Blendor,' 'Weep-no-more' and 'Why Worry?'

'To be or not to be' was the telephone number of the municipal gas chambers of the Federal Bureau of Termination.

The painter thumbed his nose at the orderly. 'When I decide it's time to go,' he said, 'it won't be at the Sheepdip.'

'A do-it-yourselfer, eh?' said the orderly. 'Messy business, Grandpa. Why don't you have a little consideration for the people who have to clean up after you?'

The painter expressed with an obscenity his lack of concern for the tribulations of his survivors. 'The world could do with a good deal more mess, if you ask me,' he said.

Answer the following note-taking questions for Fiction extract 5.

1. What is happening within the text? (Who is the character, what is happening to them, where/when is this story set?)

2. What is the implicit meaning within the text and how is this conveyed using character/plot/setting?

3. What language/structural features are used by the author to accentuate features of the character/plot/setting?

4. What other significant features or techniques do you notice?

Write a response that answers the following question, using your own notes and the sample response for Fiction extract 1 as a guide.

Practice question for Fiction extract 5

Analyse how Vonnegut invites the reader to reflect on the nature of life and death. (4 marks)

Fiction extract 6

Short story: 'How the Camel Got his Hump' by Rudyard Kipling

Now this is the next tale, and it tells how the Camel got his big hump.

In the beginning of years, when the world was so new and all, and the Animals were just beginning to work for Man, there was a Camel, and he lived in the middle of a Howling Desert because he did not want to work; and besides, he was a Howler himself. So he ate sticks and thorns and tamarisks and milkweed and prickles, most 'scruciating idle; and when anybody spoke to him he said 'Humph!' Just 'Humph!' and no more.

Presently the Horse came to him on Monday morning, with a saddle on his back and a bit in his mouth, and said, 'Camel, O Camel, come out and trot like the rest of us.'

'Humph!' said the Camel; and the Horse went away and told the Man.

Presently the Dog came to him, with a stick in his mouth, and said, 'Camel, O Camel, come and fetch and carry like the rest of us.'

'Humph!' said the Camel; and the Dog went away and told the Man.

Presently the Ox came to him, with the yoke on his neck and said, 'Camel, O Camel, come and plough like the rest of us.'

'Humph!' said the Camel; and the Ox went away and told the Man.

At the end of the day the Man called the Horse and the Dog and the Ox together, and said, 'Three, O Three, I'm very sorry for you (with the world so new-and-all); but that Humph-thing in the Desert can't work, or he would have been here by now, so I am going to leave him alone, and you must work double-time to make up for it.'

That made the Three very angry (with the world so new-and-all), and they held a palaver, and an indaba, and a punchayet, and a pow-wow on the edge of the Desert; and the Camel came chewing on milkweed most 'scruciating idle, and laughed at them. Then he said 'Humph!' and went away again.

Presently there came along the Djinn in charge of All Deserts, rolling in a cloud of dust (Djinns always travel that way because it is Magic), and he stopped to palaver and pow-pow with the Three.

'Djinn of All Deserts,' said the Horse, 'is it right for any one to be idle, with the world so new-and-all?'

'Certainly not,' said the Djinn.

'Well,' said the Horse, 'there's a thing in the middle of your Howling Desert (and he's a Howler himself) with a long neck and long legs, and he hasn't done a stroke of work since Monday morning. He won't trot.'

'Whew!' said the Djinn, whistling, 'that's my Camel, for all the gold in Arabia! What does he say about it?'

'He says "Humph!"' said the Dog; 'and he won't fetch and carry.'

'Does he say anything else?'

'Only "Humph!"; and he won't plough,' said the Ox.

'Very good,' said the Djinn. 'I'll humph him if you will kindly wait a minute.'

The Djinn rolled himself up in his dust-cloak, and took a bearing across the desert, and found the Camel most 'scruciatingly idle, looking at his own reflection in a pool of water.

'My long and bubbling friend,' said the Djinn, 'what's this I hear of your doing no work, with the world so new-and-all?'

'Humph!' said the Camel.

The Djinn sat down, with his chin in his hand, and began to think a Great Magic, while the Camel looked at his own reflection in the pool of water.

'You've given the Three extra work ever since Monday morning, all on account of your 'scruciating idleness,' said the Djinn; and he went on thinking Magics, with his chin in his hand.

'Humph!' said the Camel.

'I shouldn't say that again if I were you,' said the Djinn; 'you might say it once too often. Bubbles, I want you to work.'

And the Camel said 'Humph!' again; but no sooner had he said it than he saw his back, that he was so proud of, puffing up and puffing up into a great big lolloping humph.

'Do you see that?' said the Djinn. 'That's your very own humph that you've brought upon your very own self by not working. To-day is Thursday, and you've done no work since Monday, when the work began. Now you are going to work.'

'How can I,' said the Camel, 'with this humph on my back?'

'That's made a-purpose,' said the Djinn, 'all because you missed those three days. You will be able to work now for three days without eating, because you can live on your humph; and don't you ever say I never did anything for you. Come out of the Desert and go to the Three, and behave. Humph yourself!'

And the Camel humphed himself, humph and all, and went away to join the Three. And from that day to this the Camel always wears a humph (we call it 'hump' now, not to hurt his feelings); but he has never yet caught up with the three days that he missed at the beginning of the world, and he has never yet learned how to behave.

Answer the following note-taking questions for Fiction extract 6.

1. What is happening within the text? (Who is the character, what is happening to them, where/when is this story set?)

____

____

2. What is the implicit meaning within the text and how is this conveyed using character/plot/setting?

____

____

3. What language/structural features are used by the author to accentuate features of the character/plot/setting?

____

____

4. What other significant features or techniques do you notice?

____

____

Write a response that answers the following question, using your own notes and the sample response for Fiction extract 1 as a guide.

Practice question for Fiction extract 6

With close reference to the fiction extract, explain how children's stories are used to impart social teachings to young readers. (5 marks)

3 CHAPTER

Strategies and techniques for analysing nonfiction

In this chapter you will cover:

- **points to consider when analysing nonfiction**
- **common nonfiction features and techniques**
- **nonfiction texts: guided note-taking and practice questions.**

Points to consider when analysing nonfiction

Examples of nonfiction include opinion articles, personal essays, reviews, travel writings, creative nonfiction, memoirs, biographies, autobiographies, interviews, speeches, advertisements, letters, academic texts, journalism and historical writings. This category of text is quite broad. The common feature among nonfiction texts is that they convey information or experience based upon real facts and true events.

While nonfiction texts cite, discuss or recreate real-life events, people and experiences, it is important to note that the author of a nonfiction text may offer their own opinionated commentary upon the real-life event, person or experience explored in their writing. This will shape the reader's perception of the subject matter. For example, a nonfiction article that reports on a refugee crisis may be affected by the journalist's own opinions about human rights and politics. The author of a memoir or autobiography may be seeking to recreate their life experiences from a particular perspective, usually to garner sympathy, understanding or validation from the reader.

Here are some questions to guide your thought process when analysing nonfiction:

1. Who is the author and how close are they to what they are writing about?

How does the tone of the text reveal what the author personally feels about the subject? How informed is the author about the subject they are exploring, and how does this affect their credibility?

2. What is the intended reaction from the reader?

Types of reader reactions can be simplified into being entertained, informed or persuaded. These may intersect; however, you should be able to discern a primary purpose for the text.

3. What form is this text written in and how does this affect the author's language and style?

The text may be an online article (also see Chapter 6 of this book, on multimodal/digital texts). It may be a piece of prose writing like a memoir, essay or travel piece. If it is journalistic in style, it may have headlines, captions and capture quotes/pull-out quotes. If it is a speech or opinion piece, it is likely to contain persuasive elements like rhetorical techniques. Look for features that help you to determine the form of the text, and observe the relationship between the author's chosen form and the text's language and style.

4. What other significant features or techniques do you notice?

There are other nonfiction features and techniques (which are listed in the table below), but those mentioned in the three questions above will be the most common forms and features that you will readily identify in most nonfiction texts. You should look for these aspects first before examining other significant features.

Common nonfiction features and techniques

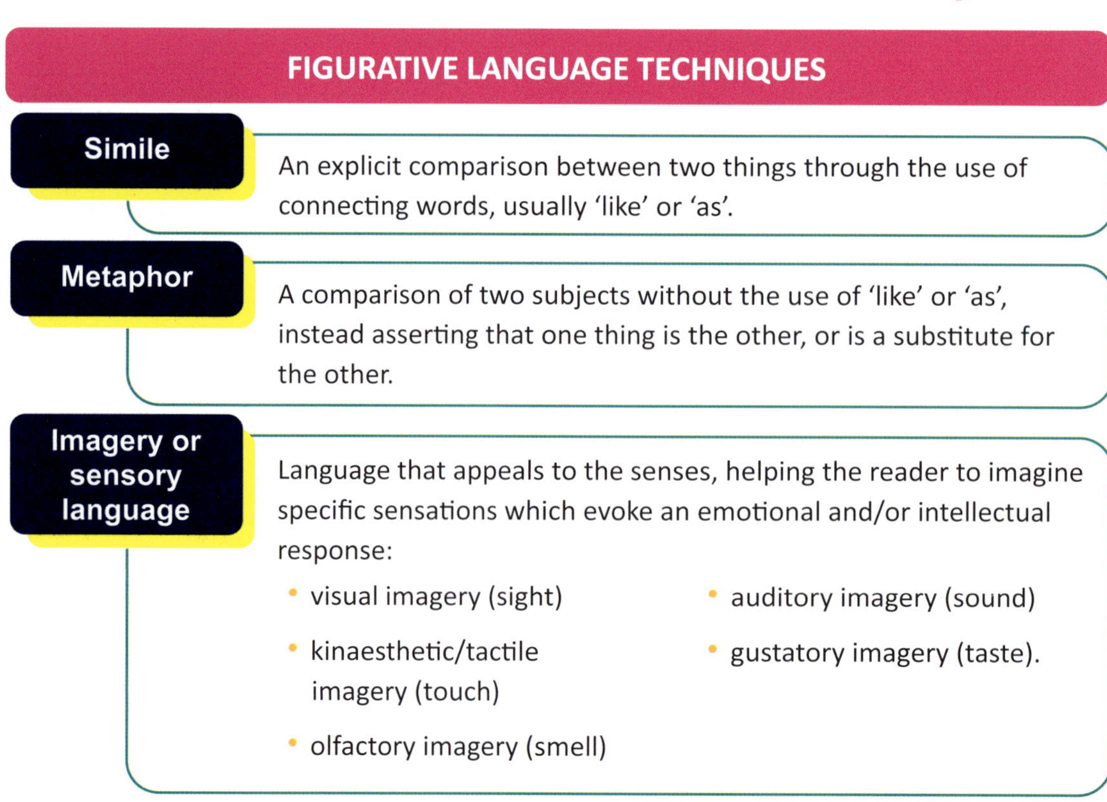

FIGURATIVE LANGUAGE TECHNIQUES	
Simile	An explicit comparison between two things through the use of connecting words, usually 'like' or 'as'.
Metaphor	A comparison of two subjects without the use of 'like' or 'as', instead asserting that one thing is the other, or is a substitute for the other.
Imagery or sensory language	Language that appeals to the senses, helping the reader to imagine specific sensations which evoke an emotional and/or intellectual response: • visual imagery (sight) • kinaesthetic/tactile imagery (touch) • olfactory imagery (smell) • auditory imagery (sound) • gustatory imagery (taste).

Symbolism

Giving objects a certain meaning that is different from their literal meaning. Writers use symbolism to tie certain things that may initially seem unimportant to more universal themes. The symbols then represent these grander ideas or qualities.

Motif

An idea or symbolically significant object or event that is repeated throughout a work of literature. Motifs may come in the form of recurring imagery, language, structure or contrasts. The development of motifs in a work of literature often contributes to mood and/or theme.

Allusion

A brief and indirect reference to a person, place, thing or idea of historical, cultural, literary or political significance. It does not describe in detail the person or thing to which it refers. It is just a passing reference and the writer expects the reader to possess enough knowledge to observe the allusion and grasp its importance and meaning in a text. When the reference is to a specific literary work, this can also be called intertextuality.

Juxtaposition

Placing two unlike things next to one another to prompt the reader to reflect on their similarities and differences.

Hyperbole

Derived from a Greek word meaning 'over-casting'. A figure of speech that involves an exaggeration of ideas for the sake of emphasis.

AURAL FEATURES

Consonance

A literary device in which a consonant sound is repeated in words that are in close proximity. The repeated sound can appear anywhere in the words, unlike in alliteration where the repeated consonant sound must occur in the stressed part of the word.

Sibilance

A special kind of consonance in which the repeated consonant sound is s, sh, z or any other sibilant sound. Sibilance occurs when the repetition of these specific consonants are in words in close proximity to each other.

Alliteration

The repetition of consonant sounds, generally at the beginning of words or the stressed parts of words in close proximity to each other.

Assonance

The repetition of vowel sounds in words in close proximity to each other.

OTHER LANGUAGE FEATURES

Feature	Definition
Emotive language	Language that elicits an emotional response in the reader.
High modality language	Language that conveys a high degree of certainty through the manner in which it's expressed.
Inclusive language	The use of pronouns (personal, possessive, inclusive) and other language that is designed to unite speaker and reader/listener in the same situation/cause/emotion.
Diction/lexical choice	The selection of a word for its particular meaning, implication or connotation. The words and style of expression that an author uses in a work of literature can have a significant effect on the tone of the text and on how readers perceive the characters.
Lexical chain	The use of a chain of words within a short segment of text which work together to cumulate meaning. For example, within a paragraph an author could use the words 'stab', 'blood' and 'screaming' which, when combined in the reader's mind, give a greater impression of violence than just one of these words would create.
Repetition	Repeating the same words or phrases a few times to make an idea clearer and more memorable.
Tone	The emotion or attitude with which something is said or written. How is the character/author feeling as they express themselves? Use adjectives to describe tone, such as 'reflective', 'regretful', 'nostalgic', 'wistful' or 'pensive'.
Mood	The emotion created by the text within the audience/reader. Mood can also be referred to as the 'atmosphere' of a text. Certain feelings are evoked in readers through words and descriptions. Mood can be developed in a text through various methods, including setting descriptions, tone and diction.
Asyndeton	The omission of conjunctions with the effect of 'piling up' references, objects or ideas (like an extended form of listing/describing). For example, 'We moved the furniture, pushed it into the corners, stacked the chairs, cleaned the rugs, mopped the floors' give the impression of hard work and busyness.

Polysyndeton

The use of several conjunctions to join connected clauses in places where they are not contextually necessary or where they could normally be omitted from a list. For example, 'The dinner was so good; I ate the chicken, and the salad, and the turkey, and the wild rice, and the bread, and the mashed potatoes, and the cranberry sauce' emphasises the variety and abundance of food and the amount eaten.

Listing

Providing numerous features to build a detailed impression or description. If this continues for a longer segment of text, it can be called **cumulative listing**.

Sentence structure

Truncated

essentially a very short sentence, often to draw emphasis to a concise concept.

Compound sentence

contains at least two independent clauses. These two independent clauses can be joined with a comma and a coordinating conjunction or with a semicolon.

Run-on

occurs when two or more independent clauses (also known as complete sentences) are connected improperly. One common type of run-on sentence is a comma splice, which occurs when two independent clauses are joined with just a comma.

Complex sentence

contains at least one independent clause and at least one dependent clause. Dependent clauses can refer to the subject (who, which), the sequence/time (since, while), or the causal elements (because, if) of the independent clause.

Simple sentence

contains a subject and a verb, and it may also have an object and modifiers. However, it contains only one independent clause.

Fragmented sentence

a string of words that does not form a complete sentence; there is a necessary component of a complete sentence missing. This missing component may be a subject (usually a noun) or a predicate (verb or verb phrase) and/or when the sentence does not express a complete idea. For example, 'Shows no improvement in any of the vital signs.'

Types of sentences

Declarative

states a fact. This word can be used to describe any action or speech that makes a statement.

Imperative

gives instructions or advice, and expresses a command, an order, a direction or a request. It is also known as a 'jussive' or a 'directive'.

Exclamatory

expresses strong feelings in the form of an exclamation.

Active/passive voice

Active voice

describes a sentence where the subject performs the action stated by the verb (e.g. 'Mary bought a lamb'). It follows a clear subject + verb + object construction that's easy to read.

Passive voice

is when the subject is acted upon by the verb (e.g. 'The lamb was bought by Mary'). It makes for a murky, roundabout sentence; you can use active voice to be clearer and more straightforward.

Irony

Verbal irony

when someone says or writes something that is in opposition to the person's true meaning. There must be some indication, however, that the speaker does not exactly mean what she or he says.

Dramatic irony

when the reader/audience of a text knows something that some characters in the narrative do not.

Situational irony

when something happens that is very different from what was expected. In cases of situational irony, there is often a twist that plays with the expectations of the audience.

Syntax

The arrangement of words into a sentence that makes sense according to the rules and principles that govern sentence structure in a given language (e.g. how words and phrases may be joined). Syntax is not a literary device as such, but rather a part of every utterance and written line. However, authors can vary syntax and make choices within these rules. Together with word choice (diction), an author's syntactical decisions can convey a certain voice and create a unique style.

RHETORICAL LANGUAGE FEATURES

Anaphora	Repeating a word or phrase at the beginning of clauses. For example, 'We will fight them on the beaches; we will fight them on the landing grounds.'
Rhetorical question	A question that creates a persuasive effect in the responder by getting them to contemplate the topic.
Anadiplosis	Repeating a word or phrase at the end of one clause and the beginning of the next. For example, 'We must eliminate poverty, for poverty leads to misery, and misery leads to despair, and despair …'
Anecdote	A personal story that has immediate relevance to the topic.
Aphorism	A short statement or observation that contains a general truth (also called a 'truism').
Aporia	Giving false impression of doubt to imply objectivity. For example, 'I don't know whether climate change is real; however, it's odd that weather patterns are …'
Hypophora	When a speaker/writer asks a question and then immediately answers it. It is different from a rhetorical question, which does not necessarily have an answer. Hypophora is often used as a way of reasoning aloud.
Tricolon	Three words, phrases or sentences – the 'rule of three' – which helps to emphasise an idea.
Understatement	Deliberately making something appear less important than it is, often in an ironic sense or to draw attention to it.

Nonfiction texts: guided note-taking and practice questions

Use the note-taking questions below to guide your thinking about each nonfiction extract, then answer the practice examination questions that follow.

Nonfiction extract 1

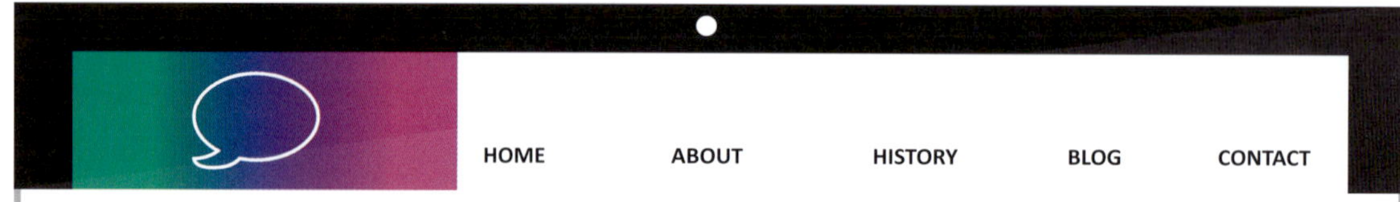

'Fatal attraction: young Australians travelling on the edge'

by David Beirman, *The Conversation*

Australians love to travel the world. In 2011 more than 7.5 million Australians (or more than one third of all Australians) travelled outside the country. Of course, most Australian travellers abroad have enjoyable visits free of danger or mishap. But occasionally, they hit the headlines for the worst reasons – they die as a result of misadventure, are victims of robbery or violent crime, overdose on drugs or as a result of alcohol-fuelled violence or accidents.

Already this year three young Australians have died in Laos, a generally peaceful destination popular among backpackers seeking an off-the-beaten-track experience. Another Melbourne teenager only narrowly escaped death.

Two of the deaths resulted from accidents incurred from 'tubing' in which people floating on an inflated tyre inner tube attempt to negotiate river rapids, often drinking at riverside bars along the way. Many of the tubers tend not to factor in sharp rocks, precipitous drops and whirlpools. Local tour operators do not provide protective clothing or head covering along the treacherous waters.

So how can you prevent young travellers from engaging in such risk-taking behaviour?

Risky fun

For Australians of all ages, but especially among the young, risk-taking is seen as an integral part of the travel experience. Great American writer Ernest Hemingway inspired adventure travellers around the world with his tales of travelling on the edge.

Each year, thousands of youthful Hemingway inspirees head to Pamplona in Spain for the annual 'running of the bulls'. Australians figure prominently among their ranks and also among those who feel the sharp end of an angry bull's horn, occasionally with fatal consequences.

Likewise, in February hundreds of young Australians gather at the Full Moon Party held at the Thai island of Koh Phangan at which they are encouraged, in fact urged by organisers, to drink buckets of spirits for the equivalent of $3 per bucket. This alcohol fueled 'party' frequently descends into drunken brawls and watery misadventure.

Taking risks abroad, free from the control of parents, is seen as a 'rite of passage' for some young Australians travelling abroad. The risks taken may range from binge drinking, drug experimentation, base jumping, mountaineering and sexual promiscuity to visiting the crime-infested, seedy districts of foreign cities.

But taking these kinds of risks can prove fatal and also costly for governments helping tourists in trouble.

Real consequences

The Australian Department of Foreign Affairs and Trade annual report reveals some rather telling statistics. In the year 01 July 2010–30 June 2011, DFAT attended to 313 arrested and imprisoned Australians overseas, 1,203 Australians who were hospitalised abroad, 12,899 missing persons and tended to over 24,000 enquiries from Australians who experienced loss or distress while overseas.

The taxpayers handed out loans totalling $325,000 to over 300 Australians who needed emergency financial assistance while abroad, most of this to cover repatriation costs.

Not so Smartravellers

Paula Ganly, Department of Foreign Affairs and Trade (DFAT)'s Assistant Secretary Consular Policy Branch, explained at a UN World Tourism Organisation conference in September 2011 that DFAT's Smartraveller campaign sought to minimise and streamline the reliance of Australian travellers on consular services through three key strategies.

The first was to urge travellers to take out travel insurance, the second was to encourage Australians to register their travel plans on the Smartraveller website and the third was to encourage travellers to closely monitor the information contained on the website about the country they intended to visit.

While DFAT's strategy makes good sense to sensible travellers, young risk-takers are hardly more likely to register their travel plans with the government than they are with their parents and DFAT's own research has borne this out.

Read the fine print

Laurie Ratz, from the Insurance Council of Australia, pointed out at the same conference that there are certain patterns of behaviour which are uninsurable. A careful fine print perusal of most travel insurance policies will show that most travel insurance providers won't cover claims from policy holders whose injuries or deaths arise from heavy drinking, drug-taking or accidents that occur undertaking unorganised high-risk activities or sport.

Many insurers will cover injuries or loss sustained for people who engage in risky activities which are part of an organised adventure tour program, sometimes at a higher premium. For travellers taking out insurance with the hope it will cover everything, it's a case of *caveat emptor*, or buyer beware. It is certainly worth taking the trouble to read the fine print.

As an extra complication, risk-taking travellers booking through internet sites can expect far less after-sales support than they would receive from traditional travel providers such as wholesale tour operators and travel agents should they need to alter their return travel arrangements while recovering from injuries sustained in taking extreme risks.

Laos tourism

In view of the tubing fatalities in Laos and the possible negative implications for the reputation of Laos as a tourism destination, the Laotian Ministry of Tourism may choose to adopt a practice used by the Tourism Ministries in many countries to license and set minimum safety standards for all tour operators engaged in 'adrenaline activities'.

This applies to such activities as bungy jumping in New Zealand. This way, those travellers who choose to engage in tubing will have an indication of those operators which operate in accordance with an agreed set of standards.

Travelling on the edge

For a small minority of travellers, taking extreme risks will always exert an attraction – even though there may be fatal consequences.

But the travel industry, government and insurance providers need to send a clear and unambiguous message to travellers that if they want to engage in extreme risk behaviour when they travel abroad, they cannot expect that the 'nanny state' they ignored will automatically spring to their rescue.

Read this example of guided note-taking for Nonfiction extract 1.

1. Who is the author and how close are they to what they are writing about? Consider their tone and credibility.

   The author sounds like a reasonably objective journalist who is writing about their area of expertise. The tone is cautionary, providing facts about tourists and risk-taking behaviour.

2. What is the intended reaction from the reader? Does thc text entertain, inform or persuade?

   The reader is prompted to reflect on or realise the ramifications of risky tourism and how it can result in unsafe situations and financial repercussions. The article seems to be both informative and persuasive.

3. What form is this text written in and how does this affect the author's language and style?

   The article is written in a mostly formal manner, aimed at an Australian audience. The article has moments of humour mixed into the informative sections which is characteristic of Australian media – for example, 'Not so Smartravellers'. Some headings have been used to structure the article.

Sample question and response for Nonfiction extract 1

Analyse how the author has used language to highlight the dangerous experiences that can occur when travelling. (4 marks)

The author has used a variety of language features to highlight how Australian tourists often engage in risk-taking behaviour which endangers their wellbeing and can end in bodily harm and financial difficulties. The headline 'Fatal attraction: young Australians travelling on the edge' highlights how tourists are metaphorically 'on the edge' of possibly fatal consequences due to their lack of regard for their own safety. The author emphasises this through listing the dangerous experiences that Australian tourists engage in as 'they die as a result of misadventure, are victims of robbery or violent crime, overdose on drugs'. This helps the audience understand the wide range of dangerous experiences Australian tourists tend to engage in, which ranges from the running of the bulls in Spain to the Full Moon Party in Thailand. The author also provided statistics in the article to help the reader understand the financial repercussions, with taxpayers handing out loans 'totalling $325,000 to over 300 Australians'. This statistic makes the reader aware of just how dangerous and financially damaging risky tourism can be.

Nonfiction extract 2

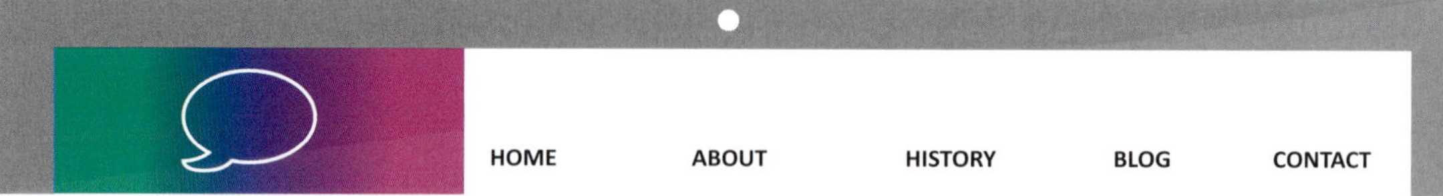

An Enquiry Concerning Human Understanding

by David Hume, published 1777

SECTION IX.

OF THE REASON OF ANIMALS.

...

83 *First*, It seems evident, that animals as well as men learn many things from experience, and infer, that the same events will always follow from the same causes. By this principle they become acquainted with the more obvious properties of external objects, and gradually, from their birth, treasure up a knowledge of the nature of fire, water, earth, stones, heights, depths, &c., and of the effects which result from their operation. The ignorance and inexperience of the young are here plainly distinguishable from the cunning and sagacity of the old, who have learned, by long observation, to avoid what hurt them, and to pursue what gave ease or pleasure. A horse, that has been accustomed to the field, becomes acquainted with the proper height which he can leap, and will never attempt what exceeds his force and ability. An old greyhound will trust the more fatiguing part of the chace to the younger, and will place himself so as to meet the hare in her doubles; nor are the conjectures, which he forms on this occasion, founded in any thing but his observation and experience.

This is still more evident from the effects of discipline and education on animals, who, by the proper application of rewards and punishments, may be taught any course of action, and most contrary to their natural instincts and propensities. Is it not experience, which renders a dog apprehensive of pain, when you menace him, or lift up the whip to beat him? Is it not even experience, which makes him answer to his name, and infer, from such an arbitrary sound, that you mean him rather than any of his fellows, and intend to call him, when you pronounce it in a certain manner, and with a certain tone and accent?

In all these cases, we may observe, that the animal infers some fact beyond what immediately strikes his senses; and that this inference is altogether founded on past experience, while the creature expects from the present object the same consequences, which it has always found in its observation to result from similar objects.

84 *Secondly*, It is impossible, that this inference of the animal can be founded on any process of argument or reasoning, by which he concludes, that like events must follow like objects, and that the course of nature will always be regular in its operations. For if there be in reality any arguments of this nature, they surely lie too abstruse for the observation of such imperfect understandings; since it may

well employ the utmost care and attention of a philosophic genius to discover and observe them. Animals, therefore, are not guided in these inferences by reasoning: Neither are children: Neither are the generality of mankind, in their ordinary actions and conclusions: Neither are philosophers themselves, who, in all the active parts of life, are, in the main, the same with the vulgar, and are governed by the same maxims. Nature must have provided some other principle, of more ready, and more general use and application; nor can an operation of such immense consequence in life, as that of inferring effects from causes, be trusted to the uncertain process of reasoning and argumentation. Were this doubtful with regard to men, it seems to admit of no question with regard to the brute creation; and the conclusion being once firmly established in the one, we have a strong presumption, from all the rules of analogy, that it ought to be universally admitted, without any exception or reserve. It is custom alone, which engages animals, from every object, that strikes their senses, to infer its usual attendant, and carries their imagination, from the appearance of the one, to conceive the other, in that particular manner, which we denominate *belief.* No other explication can be given of this operation, in all the higher, as well as lower classes of sensitive beings, which fall under our notice and observation.

85 But though animals learn many parts of their knowledge from observation, there are also many parts of it, which they derive from the original hand of nature; which much exceed the share of capacity they possess on ordinary occasions; and in which they improve, little or nothing, by the longest practice and experience. These we denominate Instincts, and are so apt to admire as something very extraordinary, and inexplicable by all the disquisitions of human understanding. But our wonder will, perhaps, cease or diminish, when we consider, that the experimental reasoning itself, which we possess in common with beasts, and on which the whole conduct of life depends, is nothing but a species of instinct or mechanical power, that acts in us unknown to ourselves; and in its chief operations, is not directed by any such relations or comparisons of ideas, as are the proper objects of our intellectual faculties. Though the instinct be different, yet still it is an instinct, which teaches a man to avoid the fire; as much as that, which teaches a bird, with such exactness, the art of incubation, and the whole economy and order of its nursery.

Answer the following note-taking questions for Nonfiction extract 2.

1. Who is the author and how close are they to what they are writing about? Consider their tone and credibility.

___

___

2. What is the intended reaction from the reader? Does the text entertain, inform or persuade?

___

___

3. What form is this text written in and how does this affect the author's language and style?

4. What other significant features or techniques do you notice?

Write a response that answers the following question, using your own notes and the sample response for Nonfiction extract 1 as a guide.

Practice question for Nonfiction extract 2

Explain the conclusions that the author draws about the similarities between animal and human experience. (3 marks)

Nonfiction extract 3

Gabrielle Carey was best known for *Puberty Blues* – but I knew her as a formidable intellectual who mastered the art of living well

by Russel Smith, *The Conversation*

The last time I saw Gabrielle Carey, who died this week, aged 64, was a couple of weeks ago in Sydney. I'd texted that I was coming to Sydney for the weekend, and she texted back to say she was meeting 'a couple of Joyceans' for a morning walk in Lavender Bay and would I like to join them?

'Joyceans' was an important code-word for Gabrielle. She is still best known as the coauthor, with Kathy Lette, of *Puberty Blues* (1979), a book she wrote as a teenager. The novel, a gritty account of the brutally sexist surf culture of Sydney's southern beaches, was a smash hit, as was the film adaptation directed by Bruce Beresford two years later. For Gabrielle, it was an early fame she would never entirely succeed in escaping.

But for many of those who knew Gabrielle later in life, she was, among many other things, a 'Joycean', and more particularly, a 'Wakean'.

She was a lifelong scholar of James Joyce, the towering Irish modernist writer whose last book, *Finnegans Wake* – a 628-page novel written in an invented language mixing the most arcane English vocabulary with more than 60 other languages in an almost unreadable riot of wordplay – is justly notorious as the most fiendishly difficult book ever written. As Gabrielle writes:

> *Wake language is a language of its own. Once you get the hang of it, Wakean words become a kind of code to share. If you're finding it hard to make a decision, you can say you're in 'twinsome twominds' and your fellow Wakeans will understand. Or if you have some gossip, you can say 'I've got a seeklet to sell.' Or if you just want to exclaim, you can invert a cliche: 'O for a fresh of breath air!' Or if someone asks why you're doing something, you can respond, 'Just for the halibut.'*

Gabrielle was an internationally respected expert on the Wake. She was in regular correspondence with the leading scholars; she was the author of numerous acclaimed essays on Joyce.

...

Her last book, currently in press, is simply titled *James Joyce: A Life*. But, by contrast with Joyce, her own style was often so modest and accessible and democratic, albeit with a fierce and fearless honesty, that it is easy to underestimate the formidable intellect at work behind her writing.

Authors were 'living beings' for her

After *Puberty Blues*, Gabrielle Carey would go on to publish nine other books, spanning fiction, biography and memoir, as well as numerous essays and newspaper pieces.

Probably her most distinctive contribution is a series of books that defy categorisation: studies of other writers that combine literary biography and autobiography, archival work and personal memoir, scholarly analysis and deeply personal reflection.

Authors were never abstract presences for her, they were living beings who breathed through their books, and it was possible to have a relationship with them every bit as passionate and dangerous as a relationship with a living human being.

The first of these was *Moving among Strangers: Randolph Stow and my Family*, a book which won the Prime Minister's Award for Non-Fiction in 2013.

Her previous book, *Waiting Room* (2009), was a searching and fearless memoir of her distant and estranged mother's terminal illness with a brain tumour, in which she briefly mentioned her mother had been friends with the reclusive Western Australian writer Randolph Stow.

In *Moving among Strangers*, she tells how she had written to Stow during her mother's last days, and that he, a deeply private man, had not only responded warmly with reminiscences of familiar family stories, but had hinted at a side of her mother's early life and personality that Gabrielle had never known existed. When she pressed him for more, he fell silent, and within a year, he had died.

Moving among Strangers tells the story of a daughter's search to find out more about her mother and the younger self her daughter never saw or knew. It's also a study of an enigmatic writer who was once internationally acclaimed, but who has now almost disappeared from Australian literary history. And it's a searching meditation on the intense relationships that can form between intensely private people.

...

When I met up with Gabrielle and her Joyceans that weekend in Sydney, we went for a walk in Wendy's Secret Garden, the garden that Wendy Whiteley, during a period of intense grieving for her husband, the painter Brett Whiteley, created on the strip of landfill alongside the railway line below their Milson's Point house.

When it began to rain, we sat under a shelter at the bottom of the garden, shouting to be heard above the sound of the rain and the clanking of hammers and screeching of angle grinders from the railway work going on a few metres away – but invisible behind the dense foliage. Every now and then the glow of an arc welder would flash through the leaves like lava breaking through rocks. When the rain stopped and we made our way back up the slope to the huge spreading Moreton Bay fig on the terrace overlooking the harbour, Gabrielle made the apology of a hostess: 'I'm so sorry about the noise, it's usually much quieter here'.

The four of us went around the corner to her friend's place and had a bite to eat and another Joycean treat, a nip of 'Aramo di Erbe', the bitter citrus liqueur made in Trieste, Italy, where Joyce spent much of his writing life. Gabrielle and I then caught the train into the city, exchanging recommendations of books to read and films to see, and when I got off at Wynyard, we embraced briefly, as you must when the train doors are closing.

When I came out of Wynyard Station, Sydney was in full torrential downpour. Instead of going to the Art Gallery of New South Wales as I'd planned, I went to the nearby Museum of Contemporary Art at Circular Quay.

There I came across the beautiful, poignant work by Simryn Gill, 'Maria's Garden' (2021), a series of life-sized ink-on-paper transfer prints of each of the plants from her neighbour Maria's garden, after Maria had died and the garden was going to be demolished by property developers.

I immediately thought 'Gabrielle will love this', and so began to see the work through her eyes, registering details I could talk about with her the next time we met. Her passion for things had that quality of enlarging your experience, making the world a richer and more beautiful place.

In her last year, Gabrielle had been taking classes in the art of bookbinding, a creative outlet to add to gardening and rose-petal jam, not to mention writing.

It was uncannily appropriate, for so much of Gabrielle's writing had been about exploring how a writer can become bound to – and bound by – the books and writers she loves.

But in addition, her writerly life was also an exploration of how books can bind readers together, bringing them closer to each other in a shared love of the beauty and power and strangeness of words.

Answer the following note-taking questions for Nonfiction extract 3.

1. Who is the author and how close are they to what they are writing about? Consider their tone and credibility.

______

______

2. What is the intended reaction from the reader? Does the text entertain, inform or persuade?

______

______

3. What form is this text written in and how does this affect the author's language and style?

______

______

4. What other significant features or techniques do you notice?

______

______

Write a response that answers the following question, using your own notes and the sample response for Nonfiction extract 1 as a guide.

Practice question for Nonfiction extract 3

Analyse how the article represents the importance of Gabrielle's storytelling to the author. (6 marks)

Nonfiction extract 4

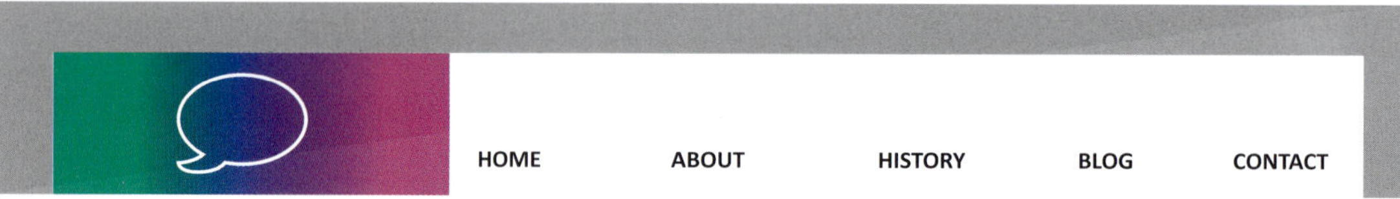

How *Alone Australia* can help us understand and appreciate our place in nature

by Lily van Eeden et al., *The Conversation*

More than a million Australians have tuned in to *Alone Australia*, SBS's highest-rating series for 2023 to date. What is it about this program that's got us so hooked? And what can it tell us about our own relationships with nature?

The series started with ten contestants dropped off in a remote area of lutruwita/Tasmania. The aim is to survive alone for as long as possible. Each contestant is relying on their ability to find food, create adequate shelter and contend with isolation from people.

Each contestant's experiences have been shaped, in part, by their unique relationship with nature. We all value and experience nature in different ways.

As armchair experts watching from home, we may reflect on how we would act if we had to survive alone in a remote place. How might our own relationship with nature shape our actions?

Nature is everywhere

Watching *Alone Australia* may generate the sense that nature, and nature experiences, happen 'out there' away from urban places and other people. This narrative has been fuelled by media, including David Attenborough's awe-inspiring nature documentaries, which paint nature and humans as separate. While this kind of media can inspire fascination with nature, it can be damaging if it perpetuates an idea that humans are separate from nature.

Nature is all around us, including in our cities. Indeed, one-third of Australia's threatened species live in cities.

This means that what urban residents (that's most of us) actually do is important for helping nature to survive and thrive. And there are many easy things we can do.

We shape nature, and nature shapes us

Your relationship with nature is part of your identity. This relationship is shaped by values, attitudes, beliefs and behaviours. It's personal and it's cultural.

Alone Australia demonstrates how humans value nature in different ways. The show helps us widen our view of valuing nature from what it provides for us (instrumental/utilitarian values) to seeing beauty and worth in nature itself (intrinsic values).

Some contestants value nature from an even broader perspective (relational values) as they reveal their deep, caring, reciprocal and even spiritual relationship with the natural world.

Previous overseas seasons of *Alone* have highlighted utilitarian nature relationships, with most contestants being white male survivalists. This season, the first in Australia, includes people from different cultures and genders, including First Nations peoples. This has highlighted different types of human-nature relationships, including spiritual and nature-as-kin relationships.

Experiences in nature early in life shape these relationships. In their 'flashback' footage, several contestants express gratitude to their parents for early experiences of nature.

For those of us with children, this might inspire us to help shape our child's 'nature identity'. Meaningful nature experiences can include looking after nature (gardening, indoor plants), bushwalks, visiting botanical gardens, or getting up close and personal with wildlife at your local zoo.

Nature as medicine

Being in nature is good for us. It might seem like the moments of awe and self-discovery in nature that we have seen *Alone Australia* contestants experience can only happen in these 'out there' places. But these experiences can happen anywhere — if we seek them out.

This will be apparent to many of us who sought solace in nature during COVID lockdowns. Connecting with nature, including in urban places, can help people feel less lonely and support their wellbeing in many ways.

For two *Alone Australia* contestants, in particular, their experiences of post-traumatic stress disorder (Chris) and the loss of a child (Gina) have been harrowing. Both describe how nature provides them with solace and healing.

For several contestants, craving connection with people was the reason to head home. Others seek kinship with nature. For example, ecologist Kate befriends her local possum family and Gina delights in regular visits by a platypus.

For First Nations man Duane, the experience strengthened his connection to Country, but experiencing that connection with family was critical:

> *It's about oneness with nature, but sharing it collectively – kindness, actions towards others, not being alone out there.*

Learning about nature

TV nature content like *Alone Australia* is educational. As the remaining contestants find food and other resources, we learn about plant and animal species and their use by the palawa people, the Traditional Custodians of the land.

This might prompt viewers to find out more about the plants and animals in their own local environments. Indeed, recent renewed interest in urban foraging has been touted as cementing our connections to place and sense of belonging.

We need nature, and nature needs us

Alone Australia highlights our complete interdependence with nature. Ultimately, everything we need for survival, including clean water, shelter and food, is derived from nature, even when we live in a city. The 'successes' of the contestants are determined by their ability to understand their relationship to the land and how to meet their basic survival needs.

If we broaden our view of nature and see ourselves as interwoven in nature's rich tapestry, as many of the contestants do, we can gain more than basic survival. We can improve our wellbeing while feeling kinship with the more-than-human, and a sense of responsibility to care for it.

Nature is in crisis, and that matters for all of us.

People who feel connected to nature are more likely to protect it. If TV nature content such as *Alone Australia* encourages us to reflect on our relationship with

nature and seek meaningful moments with nature and nature knowledge, then perhaps it might lead us to strengthen our environmental identities and act as nature stewards. And that's a great outcome for people and the planet.

Answer the following note-taking questions for Nonfiction extract 4.

1. Who is the author and how close are they to what they are writing about? Consider their tone and credibility.

2. What is the intended reaction from the reader? Does the text entertain, inform or persuade?

3. What form is this text written in and how does this affect the author's language and style?

4. What other significant features or techniques do you notice?

Write a response that answers the following question, using your own notes and the sample response for Nonfiction extract 1 as a guide.

Practice question for Nonfiction extract 4

How does the author use language to convince the reader of the intrinsic value of nature to the human experience? (5 marks)

Nonfiction extract 5

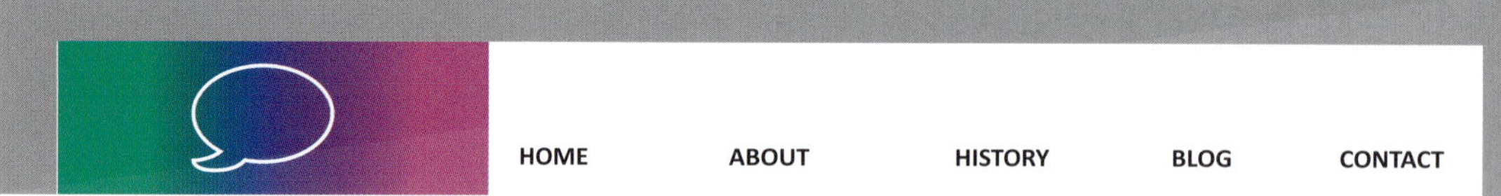

Humanity's tipping point? How the Queen's death stole a climate warning's thunder

by Darren Ray, *The Conversation*

Think back to September last year. What happened early that month? What news shook the world and reverberated for weeks, if not months?

That's a question I've been asking friends and colleagues lately.

On September 8, 2022, at 6.30pm in Britain, Buckingham Palace announced the death of Queen Elizabeth II. The news broke just 30 minutes before the press embargo lifted on a major review of climate change tipping points in the journal *Science.*

The paper in *Science* was truly earth-shattering, as it heralded changes that could threaten the future of civil society on this planet. But it was the other news that captured the world's attention.

...

Grappling with tipping points

The question of when global warming might push elements of the climate system past points of no return has come into focus over last the decade or so. And tipping points once thought to be far off in the distance have come into sharp relief.

The research examines major features of the global climate system, such as ice sheets, glaciers, rainforests and coral reefs. It asks when melting of ice sheets on Greenland and West Antarctica would become irreversible, ultimately contributing many metres to sea level. Or when thawing of frozen ground in the Arctic might start producing so much methane and carbon dioxide (CO_2) that it blows the global emissions budget.

Amazonian forest die-back is another major part of the Earth's climate system. Global heating and regional reductions in rainfall could cause trees to die, releasing large amounts of greenhouse gases. Fewer trees ultimately means less rainfall for those that remain, creating a vicious cycle.

The pivotal paper in *Science* reviewed more than 220 papers published since 2008 to estimate what level of global temperature rise (relative to pre-industrial levels) would trigger each of the global and regional climate tipping points.

...

Ice sheets in West Antarctica contain about another 3.5m of sea level rise, and again, irreversible melting is likely to begin at around 2°C.

So, that's about 5m from Greenland and another 3.5m from West Antarctica. Add thermal expansion from warming oceans, and mountain glacier melt, and we have more than 10m of sea level rise to contend with.

While that will unfold over many centuries, it will be irreversible and inexorable. It means children born today will likely see sea levels rise by well over 1m early in the 22nd century. Longer-term, these changes will shape the planet for the next 150,000 years or so, until the next ice age.

...

How did we get here?

Arriving at this juncture in human history feels like a massive failure. A failure of leadership, of decision making, of information dissemination through media, and perhaps our priorities, has left us in this extremely challenging position.

Many factors have conspired against us. These include fossil fuel companies funding misinformation and climate-related 'green washing' – exaggerating or misrepresenting their climate credentials. Elected leaders being influenced by donations from the fossil fuel industry. Earlier low-resolution climate models failing to capture local scale processes, and therefore underestimating climate system sensitivity. Poor media communication of the urgency of the issue. And throw in some good old human 'optimism bias' towards positive outcomes.

As a climate scientist, with almost 18 years experience in operations at the Bureau of Meteorology and more recently, in my work on high resolution climate projections for state government, I deeply know the climate grief so eloquently communicated by climate researcher Joelle Gergis.

In response, I have had to draw on tools such as meditation and mindfulness to deal with the awareness the science presents including the likely future suffering of so many. It is challenging to see where we are heading and – with what is at stake – to see life going on as if everything is fine.

A turning point

Future events are going to challenge us in many ways. Humanity faces a choice between retreat into fear and war, or cooperation and collaboration. There is much already happening and a lot we can do, as individuals and communities. We can restore landscapes, reward sustainability, create a circular economy and electrify everything. But we need to act fast.

So, as King Charles III's coronation plays across our TV screens and media feeds in coming days, keep the incredibly urgent climate crisis in mind. Ask our leaders to step up. Do not be distracted, as future generations will judge us for the choices we make today.

Answer the following note-taking questions for Nonfiction extract 5.

1. Who is the author and how close are they to what they are writing about? Consider their tone and credibility.

2. What is the intended reaction from the reader? Does the text entertain, inform or persuade?

3. What form is this text written in and how does this affect the author's language and style?

4. What other significant features or techniques do you notice?

Write a response that answers the following question, using your own notes and the sample response for Nonfiction extract 1 as a guide.

Practice question for Nonfiction extract 5

Explain how the text emphasises the need for humans to take action to save their world. (4 marks)

Nonfiction extract 6

André Dao's brilliant debut novel explores his grandfather's ten-year detention without trial by the Vietnamese government

By Tess Do., *The Conversation*

André Dao's remarkable debut novel began as an investigation into his paternal grandfather's ten-year detention without trial by the Vietnamese government, from 1978, three years after the war ended.

It turned into a full quest for the truth of his family history, which spans the two Vietnam Wars: the first, with occupying France, from 1946 to 1954 (the first Indochinese War); the second, 1954 to 1975 (the second Indochinese War, or the American War).

Dao was born in Australia to Vietnamese refugee parents. He's a writer, editor and artist – and a refugee advocate who co-founded Behind the Wire, an oral history project documenting people's experience of immigration detention.

His novel is not based solely on data, recorded materials and official documents: this proved impossible in dealing with repressed memory, and rendering the complexity of Dao's family story. Instead, *Anam* is a work of imagination in which the narrator tries to allow all the rival voices and conflicting versions of this saga to be heard.

From Hanoi to Saigon, Laon to Boissy-Saint-Léger, and Melbourne to Cambridge, this richly layered novel invites the reader to join Dao in disentangling different narrative threads.

Forgetting and remembering

Readers familiar with Vietnamese history will notice the peculiar spelling of the book's title: *Anam*, with one 'n'. It's a homonym of 'Annam' (Pacified South), a name imposed on Vietnam by the Chinese imperialists in the seventh century and perpetuated by the French colonialists. It refers in fact to 'anamnesis': that is, forgetting and remembering.

...

Anam is therefore not a physical place, but an imagined, mythologised 'time-place', one the narrator has created and made his own through the torturous process of writing. He connects the reader with his story, which resonates beyond the Vietnamese diaspora to touch all diasporic peoples haunted by dispossession and unbelonging. We accompany him on his journey.

Reflecting the missing 'n' in *Anam*, the book intriguingly opens with two short entries, puzzlingly labelled C and D. This points not only to the missing entries A and B, but also their recovery at the end of the novel – in the form of a series of derivatives: A, B and C.

Visually, this evokes *Anam*'s central tropes of memory loss and retrieval. It highlights the novel's painful false starts – and its completion, as the narrator attempts one last time to relate the interwoven stories of his family in three chapters, named 'Michaelmas', 'Lent' and 'Easter'.

The significance of this deliberate structure is twofold. It references the three important periods in the Catholic calendar, and the three academic terms at Cambridge University, where the narrator completes his thesis on the life story of his grandparents.

It's a *mise-en-abyme*, highlighting the embedding of one story within another, in an intricate weaving of voices that alternates between the narrator's present and his family's past. As a religious framework, it supports the narrator's endeavour to portray his grandparents through their Catholic faith.

Generational journeys

The first chapter, 'Michaelmas', refers to the celebration of Saint Michael, the saint of protection in time of peril. It's presented as an investigation that aims to piece together the grandfather's perilous journey – from his commitment to the Viet Minh cause (the Communist national independence coalition) in the 1940s, during the first Indochinese war with Vietnam's French occupiers, to his fight for survival in the infamous Chí Hòa Prison in the 1980s.

Anam inhabits the lives of real political figures such as Nelson Mandela and Trịnh Đình Thảo, a famous French-educated Saigonese attorney whose participation in the anti-war and peace movement in Vietnam landed him in Chí Hòa Prison numerous times. Their fight and willingness to sacrifice for their cause shed light on the narrator's enigmatic grandfather.

Dao's creation of a fictional Vietcong ghost in Chí Hòa Prison serves the same purpose. The grandfather and the ghost are on opposite sides in the Vietnam War and motivated by different ideologies, but as fellow inmates, they share the same suffering and the same fate.

The cover photo of the grandfather seems to suggest he's the principal character in *Anam*. But the second chapter, 'Lent', focuses on the grandmother in Laon, France.

Her story reflects the novel's themes of sacrifice, love and hope. A migrant mother, her life is characterised by her selfless care for her children and her faithful love for her husband, incarcerated in Vietnam.

Despite her willingness to talk about herself, starting with her childhood in Hanoi, her marriage and resettlement in Saigon, then her flight to France, the grandmother remains an elusive figure. The narrator feels compelled to rely on different perspectives and multiple voices to cast light on his grandmother and her life experiences.

...

A fine example of a global novel

Uncompromising and honest, *Anam* is a brilliant book of immense scope. Dao has kept the legacy of his grandparents alive through his literary creation. He raises moral questions of doubt, complicity and guilt, while showing compassion and generosity towards all choices.

The novel's themes are not uncommon in Vietnamese diasporic literature: separation of family into enemy camps, the trauma of war and dislocation, the difficulty of retrieving and representing memories, hope and renewal. But Dao handles these themes in an original and convincing way, appealing emotionally and intellectually to his reader.

Through his compelling narrative strategy, he lays bare the writing process, allowing us to take part in his experimentation with different forms and narrative styles, and transporting us across all borders: not only of geography and time, but linguistic, political and cultural boundaries.

Dao's quest to include all perspectives means both Western and Eastern philosophy and beliefs are called upon to shed light on the past. Pivotal questions of social justice and forgiveness are illuminated through the Catholic concept of God's love and mercy, but also through the Vietnamese concept of 'phúc đức', in which the forebear's moral conduct is passed on as a legacy of blessings from one generation to the next.

In terms of thematic, linguistic, and cultural scope, *Anam* is a fine example of what a global novel should be like. It beautifully connects East and West; Europe and Australasia; Oceania and the Middle East. It is an insightful addition to a series of acclaimed books on memory, war, and migration by Anglophone writers of Vietnamese origin – such as Nam Lê's *The Boat*, Viet Thanh Nguyen's *Nothing Ever Dies*, or GB Tran's *Vietnamerica*.

Dao gives us a privileged reading experience. Throughout the novel, he makes us feel the immensity of the task he has set himself – to ethically tell the story of Vietnam, of forgetting and remembering. And he makes us feel the full weight of his literary and family commitment to this project.

To use his judicious metaphor, a book on family memories is not a memorial to the past, lifeless and cold, like 'a slab of black granite'. It's a 'house with many rooms' and 'many windows': each with a different angle, each looking out on a different memory, each perspective equally valid.

Anam encourages us to reflect on the ethics of forgetting and remembering. And it inspires us to think of a way to create our own houses, from which to tell the stories of our past.

Answer the following note-taking questions for Nonfiction extract 6.

1. Who is the author and how close are they to what they are writing about? Consider their tone and credibility.

2. What is the intended reaction from the reader? Does the text entertain, inform or persuade?

3. What form is this text written in and how does this affect the author's language and style?

4. What other significant features or techniques do you notice?

Write a response that answers the following question, using your own notes and the sample response for Nonfiction extract 1 as a guide.

Practice question for Nonfiction extract 6

Analyse how the article showcases Dao's novel and 'encourages us to reflect on the ethics of forgetting and remembering'. (6 marks)

4 CHAPTER

Strategies and techniques for analysing visual texts

In this chapter you will cover:

- points to consider when analysing visual texts
- common visual features and techniques
- visual texts: guided note-taking and practice questions.

Points to consider when analysing visual texts

Examples of visual texts include artworks, comics, cartoons, graphic novels, picture books, photographs, screenshots from films and posters.

These differ from multimodal/digital texts due to their reliance on visual techniques to communicate their meaning. (Multimodal/digital texts rely on a combination of digital, visual and written techniques to convey their meaning).

Here are some questions to guide your thought process when analysing visual texts:

1. What audience is this image intended for and what is its purpose?

If it's in a picture book, it would be intended for children, with the purpose of entertaining and/or imparting moral lessons.

If it's a poster advertising something, it is probably aimed at a certain age group with certain interests with the purpose of enticing them to buy or be interested in the subject matter.

If it's an artwork or a cartoon it may be intended to make a comment or evoke a thought or emotion from a particular audience. A political cartoon, for example, would aim to prompt some reflection on a social issue or behaviour.

2. What is the salient object and what makes it salient?

Consider which object the viewer's eye is drawn to. Is this due to size and how it takes up the entire frame? Or is it salient due to a prominent colour which makes it stand out compared with the other objects in the foreground or background? Why is it significant?

3. How are colour and vectors used to create meaning?

Colour is often an important part of a visual. It can contribute to both salience and symbolism. For example, the colour red stands out because it is striking, and it can symbolise love, passion, blood or violence, depending on the composition of the visual and its other content.

Vectors, such as a horizon, the gaze of a subject, lines created by the posture of a subject, pointing fingers or actual physical lines, guide the reading path of the viewer so that they process the various parts of a visual text in a certain order. They can also contribute to salience. What vectors can you identify in the image, and how do these interact with the objects and colours used within the visual text? After processing the first feature you see, how do vectors guide your eye to the next feature of the visual?

4. Is there any symbolism?

It is likely that you have noticed some symbolic colours already, but you should also look for any symbolic objects. Symbolic meaning depends on the responder's ability to decipher how the composer intended the symbol to be interpreted, and can also depend on context.

Common symbols include:

- eyes – perception, insight into the self
- rain – sadness
- fire – destruction, rebirth
- light – hope, new beginnings, a guide
- darkness – evil, uncertainty
- mirrors – self-perception, reflection
- chains – imprisonment, union, burden.

5. What other significant features or techniques do you notice?

There are other visual features and techniques (which are listed in the table below), but those mentioned in the four questions above will be the most common visual language forms and features that you will readily identify in most visual texts. You should look for these aspects first before examining other significant features.

Common visual features and techniques:

VISUAL LANGUAGE FEATURES AND TECHNIQUES

Reading path

The path that the reader's eyes take when they process a visual text. The path moves from the most salient point of the visual text to the least salient elements. The reading path is influenced by elements such as vectors, colour and size.

Vector

A line that leads your eye from one element to another. A vector may be a visible line or an invisible one. It may be an object or part of an object (such as an arm or a leg) or an invisible line such as the direction of the gaze from a represented persons eyes to another person or object.

Salience

The salient object is the feature in a visual composition that most grabs the viewer's attention. An object can be made salient through a combination of the following factors:

- **Placement**: usually an object becomes more salient if placed towards the top and/or left of the page.
- **Colour**: the vibrancy or saturation of its colour compared with other objects or the background can make the object stand out more.
- **Size**: if it takes up the majority of the frame, an object naturally becomes salient.

Proxemics

The proximity of salient objects. This often connotes their importance to one another and/or the viewer. This term is also related to **social distance:** a close-up is intimate and creates a connection with the viewer while a long shot creates objectivity and distance.

Colour

An element that is strongly tied to our emotions. Depending on the context, it can have symbolic or evocative meanings. Placement of certain colours near each other can affect mood or draw attention to certain features.

Symbolism

The use of visual elements to signify ideas and qualities by giving them meanings that are different from their literal sense. Generally, a symbol is an object representing another object or idea and giving an entirely different meaning, one that is much deeper and more significant. Symbols do shift in meaning depending on the context in which they are used. A chain, for example, may represent a union between things or people, but it may also represent imprisonment.

Gaze

The direction in which the figure in a visual text is looking. Gaze can guide the **reading path.** There are two types:

Demand

when a figure in the visual text gazes directly at the responder. This establishes a connection between subject and viewer.

Offer

when a figure, gazes at another element within the visual text. This encourages the viewer to look at that object. The viewer is in the position of a detached onlooker.

Framing

How elements in a layout are either connected or marked off from each other and disconnected. If elements are cut off from one another they are strongly framed. Framing can be achieved by borders, and connectedness can be achieved by vectors and devices such as overlapping or superimposition of images. This technique is used most on constructed images like digital artwork, websites or magazine covers.

Foreground/ middle ground/ background

What is in the 'front' of the visual text, in the 'middle' of the visual text, and at the 'back' of the visual text. What is in the foreground is often considered more important than what appears in the background.

Juxtaposition

Placing visual elements side by side to create contrast or interaction. This could include ideas, colours, objects, figures, phrases and words.

Tone

The lightness or darkness of colours used, which can help to create a sense of depth or distance in art. Artists use light and dark colours to convey mood or emotions. Colour can be used to harmonise, or bring together elements of a visual text and create a pleasing effect; alternatively, colours can clash to evoke a more unsettled response.

The rule of thirds

A common technique for achieving balance and creating interest in compositions. If an image is subdivided into thirds both vertically and horizontally, an evenly spaced grid is created. The sections of the image where the gridlines intersect are where points of interest are often positioned.

Film techniques

These should be considered when the visual text is a photograph or a still frame taken from a film.

Establishing shot or extreme long shot – a long distance shot that establishes the setting and surroundings. The emphasis is on the background, not the subject (if any) in the frame.

Wide angle or long shot – a shot that captures all or most of the subject. The focus of the shot is the subject, not the background.

Mid shot or medium shot – a shot that captures the subjects from their head to their waist, allowing a closer examination of their body language, arms and hands.

Close-up – a shot that captures a specific detail like a subject's head or hands. This can also be applied to objects.

Extreme close-up – a shot that captures the subject in extreme detail, such as an eye, a finger or a small detail on an object.

Low/high angle shot – a low angle makes the subject look more powerful while the reverse is true when a high angle is used. A high angle makes the viewer feel a sense of power and a low angle makes the viewer feel powerless.

Eye level shot – A straight on eye level view which creates no power difference and connotes equal standing between viewer and subject.

Mise-en-scene – the arrangement of the scene, how it is staged, and what props and setting are included. For example many news shows or documentaries film people giving expert commentary in front of bookshelves to imply the experts' credibility.

Body language

Facial expressions, body positioning and gestures used to show a subject's attitudes, mood or personality.

Composition

How a visual text is made up: what it is made up of, where things are placed, how it is framed, the colour and lighting used, etc. This generally refers to the visual text as a whole.

Negative space

An artistic term that refers to the empty space between objects. This is used often in graphic design.

Contrast

Placing things that are considered opposite close to each other. Contrasts can be between colours (black and white, dark and light), sizes (large and small), shapes (rounded and sharp), textures (rough and smooth), etc. to create interest and complexity. A small contrast in colour/size/shape/texture in a visual text can also be highly salient.

Visual texts: guided note-taking and practice questions

Use the note-taking questions below to guide your thinking about each image, then answer the practice examination questions that follow.

IMAGE 1

Read this example of guided note-taking for Image 1.

1. What audience is this image intended for and what is its purpose?

This visual text is a digital composition. The subject of the image implies the value of knowledge, language and/or reading. It might be used as a decorative artwork or in advertising.

2. What is the salient object and what makes it salient?

The salient object is the book Its central, foregrounded placement, together with its dark grey colour in contrast with the bright colours surrounding it, contribute to its salience.

3. How are colour and vectors used to create meaning?

The coloured lines draw the viewer's attention as they originate from the book, implying the positive value of knowledge, reading and creativity through the composer's choice of bright, vibrant colours. The letters also form a vector that draws the reader's gaze down to the book.

4. Is there any symbolism?

There are multiple symbols – the colours, letters, hands holding the book and the book itself could all be interpreted as symbols. The symbolism associated with each of these items ensures that the viewer can see the positives of knowledge. For example, the way that the hands are grasping the book tightly and holding it up towards the viewer symbolically offers the idea that knowledge is a positive and enriching part of life for all people and something to be shared; and the black and white toning of the salient image symbolises the past, indicating that knowledge from the past is valuable and should be preserved.

5. What other significant features or techniques do you notice?

The combination of photography (arms, hands holding the book) and then the jagged shapes surrounding it draws the eye to the central placement of the book. The flow of the coloured lines and the black letters represents the abundance of information that is bursting out of the book.

Sample question and response for Image 1:

How does the image convey ideas about reading? (3 marks)

This image conveys how reading can lead to creativity and knowledge through the composer's use of colour and salience. The viewer's eyes are drawn to the coloured lines and letters before following these vectors down to the grey book. The salience of the book suggests its importance as a source of valued knowledge, while the variety of coloured lines suggests creativity. The letters are positioned to look like they have burst from the book which symbolises that language and knowledge can be gained through the act of reading.

IMAGE 2

Answer the following note-taking questions for Image 2.

1. What audience is this image intended for and what is its purpose?

2. What is the salient object and what makes it salient?

3. How are colour and vectors used to create meaning?

4. Is there any symbolism?

5. What other significant features or techniques do you notice?

Write a response that answers the following question, using your own notes and the sample response for Image 1 as a guide:

Practice question for Image 2

How does this image represent the experience of travelling? (3 marks)

IMAGE 3

Answer the following note-taking questions for Image 3.

1. What audience is this image intended for and what is its purpose?

2. What is the salient object and what makes it salient?

3. How are colour and vectors used to create meaning?

4. Is there any symbolism?

5. What other significant features or techniques do you notice?

Write a response that answers the following question, using your own notes and the sample response for Image 1 as a guide.

Practice question for Image 3

Explain how colour and vectors are used to represent the thought process. (3 marks)

IMAGE 4

Answer the following note-taking questions for Image 4.

1. What audience is this image intended for and what is its purpose?

2. What is the salient object and what makes it salient?

3. How are colour and vectors used to create meaning?

4. Is there any symbolism?

5. What other significant features or techniques do you notice?

Write a response that answers the following question, using your own notes and the sample response for Image 1 as a guide. Note that this question is worth 4 marks, requiring more textual evidence to support your answer.

Practice question for Image 4

How does this image represent ways of thinking? (4 marks)

IMAGE 5

Answer the following note-taking questions for Image 5.

1. What audience is this image intended for and what is its purpose?

2. What is the salient object and what makes it salient?

3. How are colour and vectors used to create meaning?

4. Is there any symbolism?

5. What other significant features or techniques do you notice?

Write a response that answers the following question, using your own notes and the sample response for Image 1 as a guide. Note that this question is worth 4 marks, requiring more textual evidence to support your answer.

Practice question for Image 5

Explain how this image represents human behaviours and emotion. (4 marks)

Complete the guided note-taking questions for Images 6 and 7 below before completing the 5 mark comparative question that follows.

IMAGE 6

Answer the following note-taking questions for Image 6.

1. What audience is this image intended for and what is its purpose?

2. What is the salient object and what makes it salient?

3. How are colour and vectors used to create meaning?

4. Is there any symbolism?

5. What other significant features or techniques do you notice?

IMAGE 7

Answer the following note-taking questions for Image 7.

1. What audience is this image intended for and what is its purpose?

2. What is the salient object and what makes it salient?

3. How are colour and vectors used to create meaning?

4. Is there any symbolism?

5. What other significant features or techniques do you notice?

Write a response that answers the following question, using your own notes and the sample response for Image 1 as a guide. Note that this question is worth 5 marks, requiring the balanced comparison of the two images and substantial textual evidence from both images to support your answer.

Comparative question – Images 6 and 7

Compare how Image 6 and Image 7 represent ways of discovering new human experiences. (5 marks)

HINTS:

Consider where the woman is in Image 6 and what that human experience is.

Consider the significance of the stars/galaxies, the book, where the hands are reaching, and why the composer chose a round shape within Image 7.

Refer to the beginning of the chapter for a list of other visual techniques.

5 CHAPTER Strategies and techniques for analysing poetry

In this chapter you will cover:

- **points to consider when analysing poetry**
- **common poetry features and techniques**
- **poems: guided note-taking and practice questions.**

Points to consider when analysing poetry

Poetry relies on capturing emotional experiences, often represented through abstract or figurative language.

Occasionally you may need to consider the poetic form, which includes free verse, dramatic monologues, ballads, sonnets, elegies and odes.

The personal, social and/or historical context of a poem can also be important. The name of the poet, year of publication and subject matter can indicate that the poem is targeted at a particular human experience.

HSC Examinations often utilise work by Australian poets who write about migration, refugees, national identity, the Australian landscape, Australian social issues and First Nations Australian experiences.

The poems in the HSC Examination may also draw upon general emotional experiences that are universal to all humans, such as relationships, leaving the known and travelling to the unfamiliar, pivotal moments in life when growing up, and the value of past experiences upon reflection.

Remember to consider how structural and aural features affect the mood of the poem, and how sensory language evokes images in the reader's mind. Implicit connotations in word choice and symbolism are also important elements to consider.

Here are some questions to guide your thought process when analysing poetry:

1. What is *literally* happening within the poem and what is *figuratively* being explored by the poet?

This is important to think about at the beginning of your analysis, to ensure that you understand what the poem is about and what human experience is explored or represented in the poem. For example, the persona in a poem could be literally taking a walk through a park, but the poet may be using this idea to figuratively explore the concept of aging.

2. What is the tone of the composer and/or the mood of the text?

What adjectives would you use to describe how the poet feels towards the experience they are exploring? For example, the poet may be describing the migrant experience in Australia during the 1950s, after the turmoil of World War II. Depending on the language used, you might describe the tone of the poem using words like 'anxious', 'bittersweet', 'uncertain' or 'hopeful'.

How does that tone affect you as a responder? What mood is created? Depending on *how* the poet has represented the experience of migration and what mood has been established, you might be guided to feel sympathy for the persona's hardship, or to reflect on how hardship can lead to new possibilities and hope.

3. What sensory language is used and how does this affect the representation of the human experience?

Make sure you go beyond visual imagery – there are four other senses to consider as well. Most poems will have some form of imagery, such as:

- visual imagery (sight)
- kinaesthetic/tactile imagery (touch)
- olfactory imagery (smell)
- auditory imagery (sound)
- gustatory imagery (taste).

4. What significant lexical choices (diction) or objects (symbolism/other figurative devices) stand out in this poem?

The effects and connotations of particular diction within a poem are chosen by the poet for a specific purpose. For example, if the poet chooses words that are delicate and pure, like 'pearly', 'wisps of smoke', 'mist', 'ethereal' or 'clouds', they are using their lexical choices to create a gentle, soft mood.

Symbolism is often an important feature in poetry. This could include, for example, symbolic actions like shaking hands (making peace, connecting), speaking up (expressing one's thoughts, which can be related to identity) or walking away (leaving behind an experience or discarding an old worldview).

5. How do structural and/or aural features enhance particular aspects of the poem?

Structural features, such as the repetition of a particular word or line, the way stanzas are similar or different, or whether the poem has regular line lengths until the final couplet, have an effect on how the poem is read. (Not all poetry will have influential structural features.)

Aural features relate to sound, which is often connected with the mood and tone of a poem. Consider whether devices like alliteration, assonance, sibilance or onomatopoeia make the mood of the poem soft, whimsical, harsh, nostalgic, etc.

6. What other significant features or techniques do you notice?

There are other poetic features and techniques (which are listed in the table below), but those mentioned in the five questions above will be the most common poetic forms and features that you will readily identify in most poetry texts. You should look for these aspects first before examining other significant features.

Common poetry features and techniques

FIGURATIVE LANGUAGE TECHNIQUES

Simile

An explicit comparison between two things through the use of connecting words, usually 'like' or 'as'

Metaphor

A comparison of two subjects without the use of 'like' or 'as', instead asserting that one thing *is* the other, or is a substitute for the other.

Imagery or sensory language

Language that appeals to the senses, helping the reader to imagine specific sensations which evoke an emotional and/or intellectual response:

- visual imagery (sight)
- kinaesthetic/tactile imagery (touch)
- olfactory imagery (smell)
- auditory imagery (sound)
- gustatory imagery (taste).

Synaesthesia

A figure of speech in which one sense is described using terms from another. Examples of synaesthesia are often in the form of a simile or metaphor, as this is an easy way to link two otherwise unconnected images. For example, 'the bright sound of a siren' fuses visual and auditory words together.

Symbolism

Giving objects a certain meaning that is different from their literal meaning. Writers use symbolism to tie certain things that may initially seem unimportant to more universal themes. The symbols then represent these grander ideas or qualities.

Motif

An idea or symbolically significant object or event that is repeated throughout a work of literature. Motifs may come in the form of recurring imagery, language, structure or contrasts. The development of motifs in a work of literature often contributes to mood and/or theme.

Allusion

A brief and indirect reference to a person, place, thing or idea of historical, cultural, literary or political significance. It does not describe in detail the person or thing to which it refers. It is just a passing reference and the writer expects the reader to possess enough knowledge to observe the allusion and grasp its importance and meaning in a text. When the reference is to a specific literary work, this can also be called intertextuality.

Juxtaposition

Placing two unlike things next to one another to prompt the reader to reflect on their similarities and differences.

Personification

A figure of speech in which a non-living or inanimate thing is given living, often human, attributes. The non-living object is often portrayed in such a way that we feel it can act like a human being. For example, when we say, 'The sky weeps', we are giving the sky the ability to cry, which is a human quality.

Hyperbole

Derived from a Greek word meaning 'over-casting'. A figure of speech that involves an exaggeration of ideas for the sake of emphasis.

Pun or paronomasia

A play on words that produces a humorous effect by using a word that suggests two or more meanings, or by exploiting similar sounding words that have different meanings.

Synecdoche

A figure of speech in which a word or phrase that refers to a part of something is substituted to stand in for the whole, or vice versa. For example, the phrase 'all hands on deck' is a demand for all of the crew to help, yet the word 'hands' – just a part of the crew – stands in for the whole crew.

Paradox

A statement that appears to be self-contradictory or silly, but which may include a latent truth. It is also used to illustrate an opinion or statement contrary to accepted traditional ideas. A paradox is often used to make a reader think over an idea in an innovative way.

Oxymoron

A figure of speech where two seemingly opposing and contradictory elements are juxtaposed.

AURAL FEATURES

Consonance

A literary device in which a consonant sound is repeated in words that are in close proximity. The repeated sound can appear anywhere in the words, unlike in alliteration where the repeated consonant sound must occur in the stressed part of the word.

Sibilance

A special kind of consonance in which the repeated consonant sound is s, sh, z or any other sibilant sound. Sibilance occurs when the repetition of these specific consonants are in words in close proximity to each other.

Alliteration

The repetition of consonant sounds, generally at the beginning of words or the stressed parts of words in close proximity to each other.

Assonance

The repetition of vowel sounds in words in close proximity to each other.

Onomatopoeia

Words that imitate a sound effect. These words mimic the things they are describing.

Cacophony

A mixture of harsh and discordant noises. These sounds include the plosive consonants k, t, g, d, p and b, and the hissing (sibilant) sounds ch, sh and s.

Cadence

The natural rise and fall of sound that contributes to a melodic pattern. Cadence often depends on the inflection of a person's voice and the place where a writer chooses to end a line, as well as reflecting where a line speeds up and slows down.

Internal rhyme

The use of rhyming words in the same line, or rhyming words in the middle of lines. Internal rhyme is the opposite of **end rhyme,** which involves rhyming words at the end of successive lines.

STRUCTURAL FEATURES

Stanzas
How 'paragraphs' of a poem are divided and structured. These can vary in line length.

Persona
The person from whose perspective the poem is told. This was originally a theatre technique until it was popularised in poetic form by the poets Ezra Pound and T.S. Eliot, each of whom had a few named personae from whose perspective they wrote famous poems.

Enjambment
Moving from one line of poetry into another without a terminating punctuation mark. A thought, sentence, phrase or clause does not come to an end at the line break but flows over into the next line.

Rhyming couplet
Two successive lines of poetry that have a matching end rhyme.

Refrain
A group of a few lines or a stanza that repeats throughout a poem.

Caesura
A complete stop in a line of poetry brought about by a punctuation mark. A caesura can be anywhere in a metrical line and often affects rhythm by drawing attention to particular words.

Epigraph
A short quotation at the beginning of a text or section of a text to suggest the theme of what is to come. It can be a quote from a famous person, an excerpt from or full text of a poem, or a phrase, lyric or definition. An epigraph operates as a sort of preface and can set the mood or tone for the following work.

Quatrain
A stanza in a poem that has exactly four lines. Some quatrains are entire poems in their own right, while others are part of a larger structure. Quatrains usually use some form of rhyme scheme, such as the following forms: AAAA, AABB, ABAB, ABCB and ABBA. Lines in quatrains can be any length and have any metre, but there is usually a regular rhythm to the lines as well.

Repetition
Repeating the same words or phrases a few times to make an idea clearer and more memorable.

Poems: guided note-taking and practice questions

Use the note-taking questions below to guide your thinking about each poem, then answer the practice examination questions that follow.

Poem 1

'Where They Lived' by Thomas Hardy

Dishevelled leaves creep down
  Upon that bank to-day,
Some green, some yellow, and some pale brown;
  The wet bents bob and sway;
The once warm slippery turf is sodden
  Where we laughingly sat or lay.

  The summerhouse is gone,
  Leaving a weedy space;
The bushes that veiled it once have grown
  Gaunt trees that interlace,
Through whose lank limbs I see too clearly
  The nakedness of the place.

  And where were hills of blue,
  Blind drifts of vapour blow,
And the names of former dwellers few,
  If any, people know,
And instead of a voice that called, 'Come in, Dears,'
  Time calls, 'Pass below!'

Read this example of guided note-taking for Poem 1.

1. What is literally happening within the poem and what is figuratively being explored by the poet?

The speaker is describing a place that used to look different and where they presumably lived.

2. What is the tone of the composer and/or the mood of the text?

Nostalgic, a bit bittersweet at seeing the place so different and without its 'former dwellers'.

3. What sensory language is used and how does this affect the representation of the human experience?

   Visual imagery to help the reader imagine the site of the summerhouse and the turf where they used to sit.

4. What significant lexical choices (diction) or objects (symbolism/other figurative devices) stand out in this poem?

   Time is personified in the final line.

5. How do structural and/or aural features enhance particular aspects of the poem?

   The regular line lengths create a regular rhythm. There is some alliteration and assonance. This does contribute to the nostalgic tone.

6. What other significant features or techniques do you notice?

   The poet focuses on the former occupants of this place through the use of pronouns, 'they', 'we' and naming the 'former dwellers' in the last stanza. A focus on place is established through the vivid descriptions (noted in the sensory language section for Question 3).

Sample question and response for Poem 1

How does the poem explore the impact of loss? (4 marks)

The poem explores the feeling of nostalgia and longing which is evoked by visiting a place they were familiar with in their youth. The speaker reminisces on what the place was like before using tactile imagery in the line 'the once warm slippery turf is sodden' which contrasts their past memories with their present reality. This sense of nostalgia is furthered through the juxtaposition of the 'summerhouse' being gone, 'leaving a weedy space.' This connotes how their positive memories of this place are now replaced with overgrown weeds. Time is personified in the final line, the speaker laments that, instead of a voice that called, 'Come in, Dears,'/ Time calls, 'Pass below!' This ends on a note of longing for not only the place that the speaker remembered but the people they lived with as well. Personifying time reminds the reader of how much can change, emphasising the speaker's sense of nostalgia for the people and place they once knew.

Poem 2

'As Good as New' by Henry Lawson

Oh, this is a song of the old lights, that came to my heart like a hymn;
And this is a song for the old lights – the lights that we thought grew dim,
That came to my heart to comfort me, and I pass it along to you;
And here is a hand to the good old friend who turns up as good as new.

And this is a song for the camp-fire out west where the stars shine bright –
Oh, this is a song for the camp-fire where the old mates yarn to-night;
Where the old mates yarn of the old days, and their numbers are all too few,
And this is a song for the good old times that will turn up as good as new.

Oh, this is a song for the old foe – we have both grown wiser now,
And this is a song for the old foe, and we're sorry we had that row;
And this is a song for the old love – the love that we thought untrue –
Oh, this is a song of the dear old love that comes back as good as new.

Oh, this is a song for the black sheep, for the black sheep that fled from town,
And this is a song for the brave heart, for the brave heart that lived it down;
And this is a song for the battler, for the battler who sees it through –
And this is a song for the broken heart that turns up as good as new.

Ah, this is a song for the brave mate, be he Bushman, Scot, or Russ,
A song for the mates we will stick to – for the mates who have stuck to us;
And this is a song for the old creed, to do as a man should do,
Till the Lord takes us all to a wider world – where we'll turn up as good as new.

Answer the following note-taking questions for Poem 2.

1. What is literally happening within the poem and what is figuratively being explored by the poet?

____

____

2. What is the tone of the composer and/or the mood of the text?

____

____

3. What sensory language is used and how does this affect the representation of the human experience?

____

____

4. What significant lexical choices (diction) or objects (symbolism/other figurative devices) stand out in this poem?

5. How do structural and/or aural features enhance particular aspects of the poem?

6. What other significant features or techniques do you notice?

Write a response that answers the following question, using your own notes and the sample response for Poem 1 as a guide.

Practice question for Poem 2

Examine how this poem represents the persona's emotions and memories. (4 marks)

Poem 3

'The Road That Has No End' by Joseph Burrows

Hast ever tramped along the road
    That has no end?
The far brown winding road, – your one
    Fast friend
A tattered weather-beaten swag,
    A silent mate
    To send
His dumb warm comfort to the heart,
    A fount where dreams ascend.

There's wondrous freedom on the road
    That has no end;
A man's heart glows, his spirit leaps
    To blend
Its joy of life with fierce wind's gust
    Upon his face:
    To lend
Its cry to Nature's tumult, full
    And shrill, as twilight shades descend.

The flowers bloom along the road
    That has no end
Cool breezes blow, the gum trees sway
    And bend;
The wild doves woo, and softly coo
    Their soothing notes,
    And mend
Heart's throbbing pain to sweet content,
    And peace lights on the mind's sad trend

There's pain and toil along the road
    That has no end;
A sinking heart, and weary feet
    That spend
Their strength, and lag and crave respite;
    And dim tired eyes
    That tend
To close their heavy lids upon
    The stinging dusts that upward wend.

There are sweet still hours along the road
    That has no end
'Neath twinkling stars when night's deep shades
    O'erpend;
A man's eyes shine with gathered tears,
    And memories come
    To rend
His straining heart strings, while above
    The paling lights his mood commend

I love the road, the swagman's road
    That has no end;
I love its joys, that pains and toils
    Transcend;
It is my dreams, the life that fills my heart
And when death comes and would
    My peacefulness
    Amend,
I pray that God may let my soul depart
    With my tattered swag beside me,
    'Mid my friends that never chide me,
And my face towards the distant clouded hill,
Where leads the far brown winding road
    That has no end.

Answer the following note-taking questions for Poem 3.

1. What is literally happening within the poem and what is figuratively being explored by the poet?

____

____

2. What is the tone of the composer and/or the mood of the text?

____

____

3. What sensory language is used and how does this affect the representation of the human experience?

____

____

4. What significant lexical choices (diction) or objects (symbolism/other figurative devices) stand out in this poem?

____

____

5. How do structural and/or aural features enhance particular aspects of the poem?

6. What other significant features or techniques do you notice?

Write a response that answers the following question, using your own notes and the sample response for Poem 1 as a guide.

Practice question for Poem 3

Analyse how the poet utilises imagery to invite the responder to see the world differently. (5 marks)

Poem 4

'The Walkers' by Robert William Service

(He speaks.)

Walking, walking, oh, the joy of walking!
Swinging down the tawny lanes with head held high;
Striding up the green hills, through the heather stalking,
Swishing through the woodlands where the brown leaves lie;
Marveling at all things – windmills gaily turning,
Apples for the cider-press, ruby-hued and gold;
Tails of rabbits twinkling, scarlet berries burning,
Wedge of geese high-flying in the sky's clear cold,
Light in little windows, field and furrow darkling;
Home again returning, hungry as a hawk;
Whistling up the garden, ruddy-cheeked and sparkling,
Oh, but I am happy as I walk, walk, walk!

(She speaks.)

Walking, walking, oh, the curse of walking!
Slouching round the grim square, shuffling up the street,
Slinking down the by-way, all my graces hawking,
Offering my body to each man I meet.
Peering in the gin-shop where the lads are drinking,
Trying to look gay-like, crazy with the blues;
Halting in a doorway, shuddering and shrinking
(Oh, my draggled feather and my thin, wet shoes).
Here's a drunken drover: 'Hullo, there, old dearie!'
No, he only curses, can't be got to talk. ...
On and on till daylight, famished, wet and weary,
God in Heaven help me as I walk, walk, walk!

Answer the following note-taking questions for Poem 4.

1. What is literally happening within the poem and what is figuratively being explored by the poet?

2. What is the tone of the composer and/or the mood of the text?

3. What sensory language is used and how does this affect the representation of the human experience?

4. What significant lexical choices (diction) or objects (symbolism/other figurative devices) stand out in this poem?

5. How do structural and/or aural features enhance particular aspects of the poem?

6. What other significant features or techniques do you notice?

Write a response that answers the following question, using your own notes and the sample response for Poem 1 as a guide.

Practice question for Poem 4

Explain how the poet explores anomalies, paradoxes and/or inconsistencies in male and female experiences. (5 marks)

Poem 5

'Landscape' by Charles Baudelaire

In order to write my chaste verses I'll lie
like an astrologer near to the sky
and, by the bell-towers, listen in dream
to their solemn hymns on the air-stream.
Hands on chin, from my attic's height
I'll see the workshops of song and light,
the gutters, the belfries those masts of the city,
the vast skies that yield dreams of eternity.
It is sweet to see stars being born in the blue,
through the mists, the lamps at the windows, too,
the rivers of smoke climbing the firmament,
and the moon pouring out her pale enchantment.
I'll see the springs, summers, autumns' glow,
and when winter brings the monotonous snow
I'll close all my doors and shutters tight
and build palaces of faery in the night.
Then I'll dream of blue-wet horizons,
weeping fountains of alabaster, gardens,
kisses, birdsong at morning or twilight,
all in the Idyll that is most childlike.
The mob that are beating in vain on the glass,
won't make me raise my head as they pass.
Since I'll be plunged deep in the thrill
of evoking the springtime through my own will,
raising the sun out of my own heart,
making sweet air from my burning thought.

Answer the following note-taking questions for Poem 5.

1. What is literally happening within the poem and what is figuratively being explored by the poet?

2. What is the tone of the composer and/or the mood of the text?

3. What sensory language is used and how does this affect the representation of the human experience?

4. What significant lexical choices (diction) or objects (symbolism/other figurative devices) stand out in this poem?

5. How do structural and/or aural features enhance particular aspects of the poem?

6. What other significant features or techniques do you notice?

Write a response that answers the following question, using your own notes and the sample response for Poem 1 as a guide.

Practice question for Poem 5

Explain how the poet invites the reader into his creative process ('in order to write my chaste verses'). (4 marks)

Poem 6

'Ambition and Art' by AB ('Banjo') Paterson

Ambition

I am the maid of the lustrous eyes
Of great fruition,
Whom the sons of men that are over-wise
Have called Ambition.

And the world's success is the only goal
I have within me;
The meanest man with the smallest soul
May woo and win me.

For the lust of power and the pride of place
To all I proffer.
Wilt thou take thy part in the crowded race
For what I offer?

The choice is thine, and the world is wide –
Thy path is lonely.
I may not lead and I may not guide –
I urge thee only.

I am just a whip and a spur that smites
To fierce endeavour.
In the restless days and the sleepless nights
I urge thee ever.

Thou shalt wake from sleep with a startled cry,
In fright unleaping
At a rival's step as it passes by
Whilst thou art sleeping.

Honour and truth shall be overthrown
In fierce desire;
Thou shalt use thy friend as a stepping-stone
To mount thee higher.

When the curtain falls on the sordid strife
That seemed so splendid,
Thou shalt look with pain on the wasted life
That thou hast ended.

Thou hast sold thy life for a guerdon small
In fitful flashes;
There has been reward – but the end of all
Is dust and ashes.

For the night has come and it brings to naught
Thy projects cherished,
And thine epitaph shall in brass be wrought –
'He lived, and perished.'

Art

I wait for thee at the outer gate,
My love, mine only;
Wherefore tarriest thou so late
While I am lonely?

Thou shalt seek my side with a footstep swift;
In thee implanted
Is the love of Art and the greatest gift
That God has granted.

And the world's concerns with its rights and wrongs
Shall seem but small things –
Poet or painter, or singer of songs,
Thine art is all things.

For the wine of life is a woman's love
To keep beside thee;
But the love of Art is a thing above –
A star to guide thee.

As the years go by with the love of Art
All undiminished,
Thou shalt end thy days with a quiet geart –
Thy work is finished.

So the painter fashions a picture strong
That fadeth never,
And the singer singeth a wondrous song
That lives for ever.

Answer the following note-taking questions for Poem 6.

1. What is literally happening within the poem and what is figuratively being explored by the poet?

2. What is the tone of the composer and/or the mood of the text?

3. What sensory language is used and how does this affect the representation of the human experience?

4. What significant lexical choices (diction) or objects (symbolism/other figurative devices) stand out in this poem?

5. How do structural and/or aural features enhance particular aspects of the poem?

6. What other significant features or techniques do you notice?

Write a response that answers the following question, using your own notes and the sample response for Poem 1 as a guide.

Practice question for Poem 6

Analyse how the poet represents the relationship between art and artist. (4 marks)

Using your notes for Poem 5 and 6, write a response that answers the following comparative question. Remember that you can reuse your previous quotes and techniques. Note that this question is worth 6 marks, requiring the balanced comparison of the two poems and substantial textual evidence from both texts to support your answer.

Practice question for Poem 5 and 6

Compare how Baudelaire and Paterson represent the connection between the world and artistic inspiration. (6 marks)

6 CHAPTER Strategies and techniques for multimodal/digital texts

In this chapter you will cover:

- points to consider when analysing multimodal/digital texts
- common multimodal/digital features and techniques
- multimodal/digital texts: guided note-taking and practice questions.

Points to consider when analysing multimodal/digital texts

Examples of multimodal/digital texts include websites, blogs, advertisements, graphic novels, articles, multimedia compositions and book covers.

These texts rely on a combination of words and images which are deliberately constructed to create meaning. When you look at these texts, you will be observing and analysing many of the same techniques that you have looked at in the fiction, nonfiction and visual text sections of this workbook.

Here are some questions to guide your thought process when analysing multimodal/digital texts:

1. Was this composed to inform, persuade or entertain? Who is the audience?

This text type has a wide range of forms, which means that it is extremely important to discern the intended audience and its impact. A travel blog would be a combination of informing, persuading and entertaining, since it would be written to share the personal experiences of the writer as well as promote certain aspects of travel or the country that was visited. A graphic novel would be aimed more towards entertaining with perhaps an

undercurrent of persuasion, depending on the age of its audience. An opinion article may be aimed at an older audience with the intention of persuading the reader to consider the writer's opinion and reflect on their own assumptions about or view of the world.

2. What is the subject matter and what components has the composer used to explore it?

The phrasing of this part is deliberately vague due to the nature of multimodal/digital texts. There will always be subject matter; the way the composer chooses to explore that subject matter could be direct or indirect. The examples or components they choose to help make their point could be figurative or literal. For example, imagine an online article that sets out to focus on political apathy. It could do this by focusing on the actions of the government and society during the COVID-19 pandemic. Taking the same subject matter but using very different components, a satirical cartoonist may create a cartoon strip that also focuses on political apathy but represents issues allegorically by substituting animals for humans to represent different political figures.

3. How is the responder positioned to think and feel by the end of the text?

The word choice and tone of the text will guide you towards what the composer's attitudes, feelings and ideas are. Look for key lines and consider the intended response from the responder. What are you guided to think about or consider throughout the text, and what final thoughts and feelings are you left with by the conclusion of the text? You should think about what adjectives you would use to describe this. For example, you could be taken aback by new information the author is revealing about historical incidents and, by the time you finish, you could be contemplating your own responsibility in acknowledging your nation's past atrocities. Alternatively, you could be amused by the new perspective the author is sharing and finish with an affirmed view that the simple things in life should be appreciated.

4. What are the main visual and language techniques? How are they combined/ structured to convey meaning?

Multimodal/digital compositions will have specific formatting depending on what form that take: for example, headlines, subheadings, captions, images, photographs, capture quotes, etc. How are these components chosen and structured to guide the responder by the conclusion of the text? How do these connect to the final message/ideas.

5. What other significant features or techniques do you notice?

To help you decide which features and techniques to focus on, consider whether the text is more focused on engaging the responder through emotion, logic or a combination of both. Aside from helping you discern the meaning of the text, this will also help you narrow down which techniques you should be identifying and analysing in a text. The table below lists many of the techniques that you will encounter in multimodal/digital texts.

Common multimodal/digital features and techniques

VISUAL TECHNIQUES

Salience

The salient object is the feature in a visual composition that most grabs the viewer's attention. An object can be made salient through a combination of the following factors:

Placement
usually an object becomes more salient if placed towards the top and/or left of the page.

Colour
the vibrancy or saturation of its colour compared with other objects or the background can make the object stand out more.

Size
if it takes up the majority of the frame, an object naturally becomes salient.

Proxemics

The proximity of salient objects. This often connotes their importance to one another and/or the viewer. This term is also related to **social distance**: a close-up is intimate and creates a connection with the viewer, while a long shot creates objectivity and distance.

Colour

An element that is strongly tied to our emotions. Depending on the context, it can have symbolic or evocative meanings. Placement of certain colours near each other can affect mood or draw attention to certain features.

Symbolism

The use of visual elements to signify ideas and qualities by giving them meanings that are different from their literal sense. Generally, a symbol is an object representing another object or idea and giving an entirely different meaning, one that is much deeper and more significant. Symbols do shift in meaning depending on the context in which they are used. A chain, for example, may represent a union between things or people, but it may also represent imprisonment.

Juxtaposition

Placing visual elements side by side to create contrast or interaction. This could include ideas, colours, objects, figures, phrases and words.

Tone

The lightness or darkness of colours used, which can help to create a sense of depth or distance in art. Artists use light and dark colours to convey mood or emotions. Colour can be used to harmonise, or bring together, elements of a visual text and create a pleasing effect; alternatively, colours can clash to evoke a more unsettled response.

Film techniques

These should be considered when the visual text is a photograph or a still frame taken from a film.

Establishing shot or extreme long shot – a long distance shot that establishes the setting and surroundings. The emphasis is on the background, not the subject (if any) in the frame.

Wide angle or long shot – a shot that captures all or most of the subject. The focus of the shot is the subject, not the background.

Mid shot or medium shot – a shot that captures the subjects from their head to their waist, allowing a closer examination of their body language, arms and hands.

Close-up – a shot that captures a specific detail like a subject's head or hands. This can also be applied to objects.

Extreme close-up – a shot that captures the subject in extreme detail, such as an eye, a finger or a small detail on an object.

Low/high angle shot – a low angle makes the subject look more powerful while the reverse is true when a high angle is used. A high angle makes the viewer feel a sense of power and a low angle makes the viewer feel powerless.

Eye level shot – A straight on eye level view which creates no power difference and connotes equal standing between viewer and subject.

Mise-en-scene – the arrangement of the scene, how it is staged, and what props and setting are included. For example many news shows or documentaries film people giving expert commentary in front of bookshelves to imply the experts' credibility.

Composition

How a visual text is made up: what it is made up of, where things are placed, how it is framed, the colour and lighting used, etc. This generally refers to the visual text as a whole.

Contrast

Placing things that are considered opposite close to each other. Contrasts can be between colours (black and white, dark and light), sizes (large and small), shapes (rounded and sharp), textures (rough and smooth), etc. to create interest and complexity. A small contrast in colour/size/shape/texture in a visual text can also be highly salient.

FIGURATIVE LANGUAGE TECHNIQUES

Simile

An explicit comparison between two things through the use of connecting words, usually 'like' or 'as'.

Metaphor

A comparison of two subjects without the use of 'like' or 'as', instead asserting that one thing is the other, or is a substitute for the other.

Imagery or sensory language

Language that appeals to the senses, helping the reader to imagine specific sensations which evoke an emotional and/or intellectual response:

- visual imagery (sight)
- kinaesthetic/tactile imagery (touch)
- olfactory imagery (smell)
- auditory imagery (sound)
- gustatory imagery (taste).

Symbolism

Giving objects a certain meaning that is different from their literal meaning. Composers use symbolism to tie certain things that may initially seem unimportant to more universal themes. The symbols then represent these grander ideas or qualities.

Motif

An idea or symbolically significant object or event that is repeated throughout a work of literature. Motifs may come in the form of recurring imagery, language, structure or contrasts. The development of motifs in a work of literature often contributes to mood and/or theme.

Allusion

A brief and indirect reference to a person, place, thing or idea of historical, cultural, literary or political significance. It does not describe in detail the person or thing to which it refers. It is just a passing reference and the writer expects the reader to possess enough knowledge to observe the allusion and grasp its importance and meaning in a text. When the reference is to a specific literary work, this can also be called intertextuality.

Juxtaposition

Placing two unlike things next to one another to prompt the reader to reflect on their similarities and differences.

Hyperbole

Derived from a Greek word meaning 'over-casting'. A figure of speech that involves an exaggeration of ideas for the sake of emphasis.

AURAL FEATURES

Consonance

A literary device in which a consonant sound is repeated in words that are in close proximity. The repeated sound can appear anywhere in the words, unlike in alliteration where the repeated consonant sound must occur in the stressed part of the word.

Sibilance

A special kind of consonance in which the repeated consonant sound is s, sh, z or any other sibilant sound. Sibilance occurs when the repetition of these specific consonants are in words in close proximity to each other.

Alliteration

The repetition of consonant sounds, generally at the beginning of words or the stressed parts of words in close proximity to each other

Assonance

The repetition of vowel sounds in words in close proximity to each other.

Onomatopoeia

Words that imitate a sound effect. These words mimic the things they are describing.

OTHER LANGUAGE FEATURES

Emotive language	Language that elicits an emotional response in the reader.
High modality language	Language that conveys a high degree of certainty through the manner in which it's expressed.
Inclusive language	The use of pronouns (personal, possessive, inclusive) and other language that is designed to unite speaker and reader/listener in the same situation/cause/emotion.
Diction/lexical choice	The selection of a word for its particular meaning, implication or connotation. The words and style of expression that an author uses in a work of literature can have a significant effect on the tone of the text and on how readers perceive the characters.
Lexical chain	The use of a chain of words within a short segment of text which work together to cumulate meaning. For example, within a paragraph an author could use the words 'stab', 'blood' and 'screaming' which, when combined in the reader's mind, give a greater impression of violence than just one of these words would create.
Repetition	Repeating the same words or phrases a few times to make an idea clearer and more memorable.
Tone	The emotion or attitude with which something is said or written. How is the character/author feeling as they express themselves? Use adjectives to describe tone, such as 'reflective', 'regretful', 'nostalgic', 'wistful' or 'pensive'.
Mood	The emotion created by the text within the audience/reader. Mood can also be referred to as the 'atmosphere' of a text. Certain feelings are evoked in readers through words and descriptions. Mood can be developed in a text through various methods, including setting descriptions, tone and diction.

Asyndeton

The omission of conjunctions with the effect of 'piling up' references, objects or ideas (like an extended form of listing/describing). For example, 'We moved the furniture, pushed it into the corners, stacked the chairs, cleaned the rugs, mopped the floors' gives the impression of hard work and busyness.

Polysyndeton

The use of several conjunctions to join connected clauses in places where they are not contextually necessary or where they could normally be omitted from a list. For example, 'The dinner was so good; I ate the chicken, and the salad, and the turkey, and the wild rice, and the bread, and the mashed potatoes, and the cranberry sauce' emphasises the variety and abundance of food and the amount eaten.

Listing

Providing numerous features to build a detailed impression or description. If this continues for a longer segment of text, it can be called **cumulative listing**.

Sentence structure

Truncated

essentially a very short sentence, often to draw emphasis to a concise concept.

Run-on

occurs when two or more independent clauses (also known as complete sentences) are connected improperly. One common type of run-on sentence is a comma splice, which occurs when two independent clauses are joined with just a comma.

Simple sentence

contains a subject and a verb, and it may also have an object and modifiers. However, it contains only one independent clause.

Compound sentence
contains at least two independent clauses. These two independent clauses can be joined with a comma and a coordinating conjunction or with a semicolon.

Complex sentence
contains at least one independent clause and at least one dependent clause. Dependent clauses can refer to the subject (who, which), the sequence/time (since, while), or the causal elements (because, if) of the independent clause.

Fragmented sentence
a string of words that does not form a complete sentence; there is a necessary component of a complete sentence missing. This missing component may be a subject (usually a noun) or a predicate (verb or verb phrase) and/or when the sentence does not express a complete idea. For example, 'Shows no improvement in any of the vital signs.'

Types of sentences

Declarative
states a fact. This word can be used to describe any action or speech that makes a statement.

Imperative
gives instructions or advice, and expresses a command, an order, a direction or a request. It is also known as a 'jussive' or a 'directive'.

Exclamatory
expresses strong feelings in the form of an exclamation.

Active/passive voice

Active voice
describes a sentence where the subject performs the action stated by the verb (e.g. 'Mary bought a lamb'). It follows a clear subject + verb + object construction that's easy to read.

Passive voice
is when the subject is acted upon by the verb (e.g. 'The lamb was bought by Mary'). It makes for a murky, roundabout sentence; you can use active voice to be clearer and more straightforward.

Irony

Verbal irony

when someone says or writes something that is in opposition to the person's true meaning. There must be some indication, however, that the speaker does not exactly mean what she or he says.

Dramatic irony

when the reader/audience of a text knows something that some characters in the narrative do not.

Situational irony

when something happens that is very different from what was expected. In cases of situational irony, there is often a twist that plays with the expectations of the audience.

Syntax

The arrangement of words into a sentence that makes sense according to the rules and principles that govern sentence structure in a given language (e.g. how words and phrases may be joined). Syntax is not a literary device as such, but rather a part of every utterance and written line. However, authors can vary syntax and make choices within these rules. Together with word choice (diction), an author's syntactical decisions can convey a certain voice and create a unique style.

RHETORICAL LANGUAGE FEATURES

Anaphora

Repeating a word or phrase at the beginning of clauses. For example, 'We will fight them on the beaches; we will fight them on the landing grounds.'

Rhetorical question

A question that creates a persuasive effect in the responder by getting them to contemplate the topic.

Anadiplosis

Repeating a word or phrase at the end of one clauses and the beginning of the next. For example, 'We must eliminate poverty, for poverty leads to misery, and misery leads to despair, and despair …'

Anecdote

A personal story that has immediate relevance to the topic.

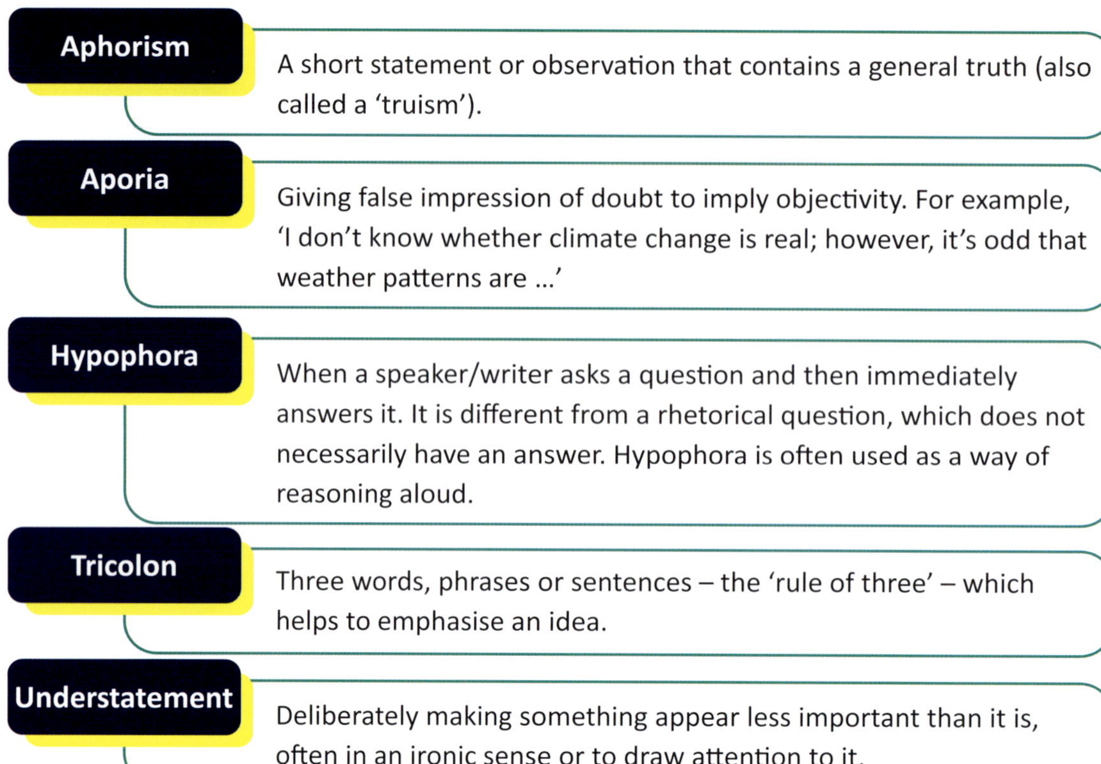

Aphorism
A short statement or observation that contains a general truth (also called a 'truism').

Aporia
Giving false impression of doubt to imply objectivity. For example, 'I don't know whether climate change is real; however, it's odd that weather patterns are ...'

Hypophora
When a speaker/writer asks a question and then immediately answers it. It is different from a rhetorical question, which does not necessarily have an answer. Hypophora is often used as a way of reasoning aloud.

Tricolon
Three words, phrases or sentences – the 'rule of three' – which helps to emphasise an idea.

Understatement
Deliberately making something appear less important than it is, often in an ironic sense or to draw attention to it.

Multimodal/digital texts: guided note-taking and practice questions

Use the note-taking questions below to guide your thinking about each multimedia/digital extract, then answer the practice examination questions that follow.

Multimodal/digital extract 1

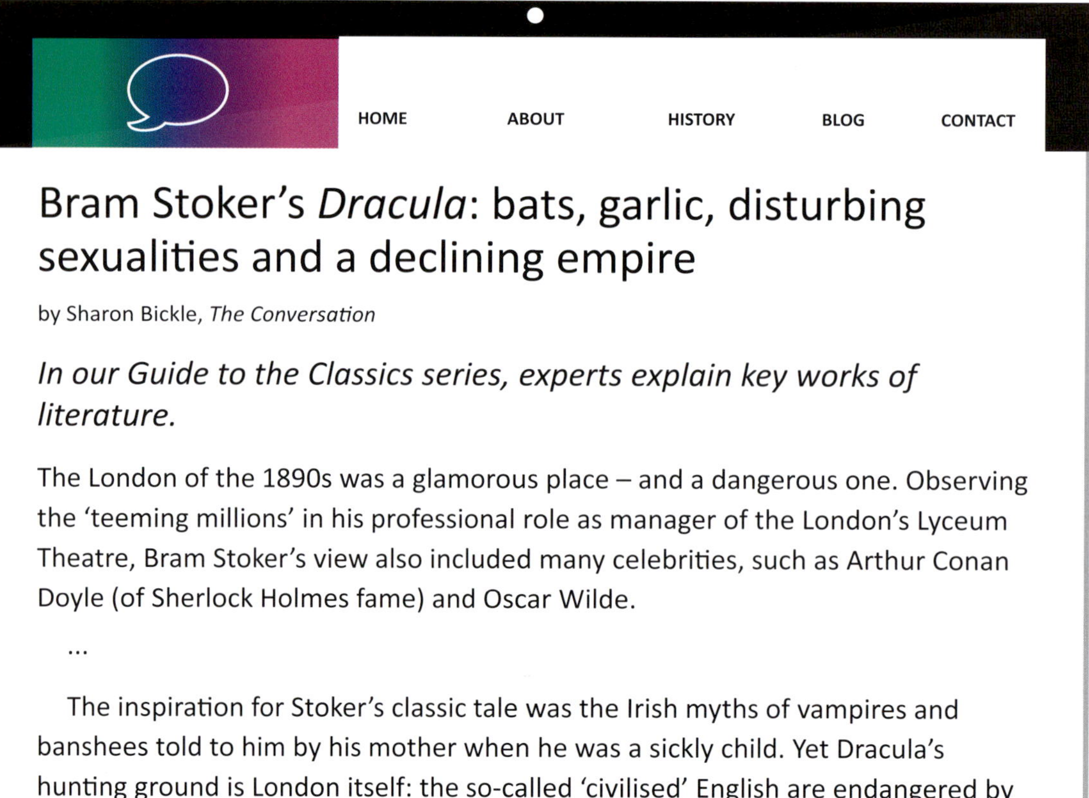

HOME ABOUT HISTORY BLOG CONTACT

Bram Stoker's *Dracula*: bats, garlic, disturbing sexualities and a declining empire

by Sharon Bickle, *The Conversation*

In our Guide to the Classics series, experts explain key works of literature.

The London of the 1890s was a glamorous place – and a dangerous one. Observing the 'teeming millions' in his professional role as manager of the London's Lyceum Theatre, Bram Stoker's view also included many celebrities, such as Arthur Conan Doyle (of Sherlock Holmes fame) and Oscar Wilde.

...

The inspiration for Stoker's classic tale was the Irish myths of vampires and banshees told to him by his mother when he was a sickly child. Yet Dracula's hunting ground is London itself: the so-called 'civilised' English are endangered by their own modernity, and made vulnerable because of their overconfident belief in rationality and the superiority of race and nation.

Claes Bang in a 2020 adaptation of Dracula , *Hartswood Films, BBC, Netflix/idmb*

...

Sexual transgression

Stoker uses the vampire to explore the cultural perils surrounding him. By the 1890s, Britain feared its empire was in decline – threatened by foreigners without and communities of migrants within. As London grew, diseases like cholera struck suddenly, and ravaged the metropolis.

And there were fears of moral contamination. Liberated 'New Women' sought jobs, rights, and the vote. Homosexual scandals erupted in the press, culminating in the 1895 trial and imprisonment of Oscar Wilde. Dracula's monstrosity threatens to uncover the frailty of Britain's imperial mastery and – as with Harker – its masculinity.

Gary Oldman and Winona Ryder in a 1992 film of Dracula. *American Zoetrope, Columbia Pictures, Osiris Films*

...

Between myth and parody

Arriving at roughly the same time as early experiments with film, Dracula quickly became synonymous with horror films. First played by Bela Lugosi and Christopher Lee, Dracula is endlessly adapted. The vampire is now ubiquitous in popular culture.

The uncanny – familiar objects behaving in unfamiliar ways – lies at the heart of horror. But today's Dracula narrative is often diluted by its familiarity. Sanitised versions of the vampire abound. Children meet 'Drac' through *Sesame Street's* The

Count, or the character voiced by Adam Sandler in *Hotel Transylvania*. These vampires' obsessions are maths and domestic fatherhood – nary a drop of blood in sight.

Comic and campy versions have repositioned Dracula as part of the harmless family fun of Halloween – from Grandpa in *The Munsters*, to Nandor the Relentless in the mockumentary, *What We Do in the Shadows*. If the best way to deal with our worst fears is to render them ridiculous, then perhaps these parodies still speak to the power of Stoker's original vision, and the unconscious fears it taps.

For every spoof, there is another story of the vampire as the predator in the darkness or the monster inside our home – including the genuinely unsettling vampire film, *Let the Right One In*.

And Dracula continues to be an effective allegory for our worst social and cultural fears. In the 1980s, the vampire's association with blood and sexual transgression made it perfect for exploring the AIDS crisis. More recently, in series like *True Blood*, vampire stories have explored the demonisation of social minorities and difference.

The gothic revival

Gothic stories emerged in the tumult of the late 18th century. But, as gothic critic, Kelly Hurley observes: 'the Gothic is rightly, if partially, understood as a cyclical genre that reemerges in times of cultural stress.'

At the turn of the 20th century, the British were gripped by cultural uncertainty. Literary scholar Stephen Arata has identified a fear of enervation at this time: 'the sense that the entire nation – as a race of people, as a political and imperial force, as a social and cultural power – was in irretrievable decline.'

This led to the gothic revival, during which our most popular (and persistent) gothic stories emerged: *Dr Jekyll and Mr Hyde*, *The Picture of Dorian Gray*, and the return of the vampire in *Dracula*.

Gothic stories excite the senses, relying on our preconditioned responses to common textual elements: castles, ruined abbeys, storms, uncanny doubles to evoke terror. Stoker uses these gothic tropes to heighten expectation.

...

Technological change

Victorian inventions like the typewriter, the telegram and the railway now seem slow and outdated. But they were the cutting-edge technologies of Stoker's day.

Van Helsing declares to his fellow vampire-hunters:

> *[W]e have sources of science; we are free to act and think; and the hours of the day and the night are ours equally. In fact, so far as our powers extend, they are unfettered, and we are free to use them.*

Dracula relies on the old ways – carriages, sailing ships, and letters. His pursuers use shorthand, wax cylinders for voice recordings and the typewriter, enabling them to collate and share information: the power of mass media. Ultimately, it is technology that defeats Dracula.

...

Threatening sexuality

English fears of homosexuality peaked with the trials of Oscar Wilde, who Stoker knew well. Indeed, author and scholar Talia Schaffer argues Stoker's passionate admiration for Walt Whitman displays a homoerotic intensity.

Lurking in the novel's shadows is the question of what happened between Harker and Dracula in Carpathia? Harker's experiences leave him shattered in mind and body. Sister Agatha reports, 'the traces of such an illness as his do not lightly die away.'

Dracula's at-arm's-length condemnation of homosexuality is almost certainly influenced by the timing of its composition, so close to Wilde's conviction for gross indecency. Perhaps, like many of Wilde's former friends and associates, Stoker wanted to signal his distance from Wilde and his scandalous lifestyle.

Dracula's defeat promises resolution. But the birth of baby Quincey Harker, whose 'bundle of names links all our little band of men together', reminds us of Mina's exclusion from the band. It recalls her sharing blood with Dracula – and echoes Lucy's promiscuous desire for three husbands. Questions of racial contamination and England's fate are left open.

Dracula, as gothic monster, represents turn-of-the-century fears of immigrants, of modern technology, of Jews, of women's rights, of homosexuality. Yet, 125 years later, Stoker's creation continues to target our deepest fears.

Read this example of guided note-taking process for Multimodal/digital extract 1.

1. Was this composed to inform, persuade or entertain? Who is the audience?

This article seems like a mixture between informing the reader of the role of Dracula and the gothic genre in society and persuading them that gothic tales have an enduring relevance. This seems targeted at the everyday, intelligent reader.

2. What is the subject matter and what components has the composer used to explore it?

The gothic monster and how it represents a society's anxieties. The author has chosen to focus on the character of Dracula as her main example, comparing and contrasting different versions and influences on Dracula's representation.

3. How is the responder positioned to think and feel by the end of the text?

The responder is introduced to the original ideas from Dracula and how they were born out of contextual anxieties. By the end of the text, the responder is reflecting on the complexities of Dracula as a character and how gothic texts and representations of Dracula still reveal humanity's fears.

4. What are the main visual and language techniques. How are they combined/structured to convey meaning?

The author uses many intertextual references and academic references to enhance her credibility. The author swaps between high modality when emphasising key points and low modality/rhetorical questions when she wants the responder to reflect on an idea. There are various visual elements that complement the author's focus on representations of Dracula over time, and the headline is a succinct summary of what she wants the responder to focus on: how the story of Dracula can be deconstructed to reveal the society and culture it was born from.

5. What other significant features or techniques do you notice?

Asyndeton is used in the final paragraph to emphasise the extensive list of fears that were felt by audiences of the past and are shared by audiences of today. Dracula, as gothic monster, represents turn-of-the-century fears of immigrants, of modern technology, of Jews, of women's rights, of homosexuality.

Sample question and responses for Multimodal/digital extract 1

(Note: There are two sample responses for this question, given the wide range of visual and language features you need to choose from when analysing a multimodal/digital text.)

How does the article highlight the power of storytelling in capturing particular cultures across time? (4 marks)

Response 1

The article highlights how vampire stories can capture society's anxieties across time, whether it's the original Dracula *from 1897 or the more recent vampiric stories told in the 20th century. The author references the socio historical context by listing sources of 'moral contamination' such as 'liberated 'New Women',' 'homosexual scandals' and 'the 1895 trial and imprisonment of Oscar Wilde.' These references demonstrate the author's argument that vampiric stories can be deconstructed to reveal what society fears.*

The subheading 'Between myth and parody' helps to develop the author's point about the vampire figure representing societal anxieties, this time switching to more recent examples in children's films and more comic representations. The author argues that 'the best way to deal with our worst fears is to render them ridiculous', using inclusive language ('our worst fears') to emphasise that this is a shared experience, with vampire stories across time being utilised to confront society's fears of difference.

Response 2

The article highlights how vampire stories can capture society's anxieties across time, whether it's the original Dracula *from 1897 or the more recent vampiric stories told in the 20th century. The second image taken from the 1992 film shows the female in a submissive pose, helpless in Dracula's dominant grip which helps to accentuate the 'disturbing sexualities' and the unease society feels towards the sexually aggressive vampire figure. This establishes the author's focus on the validity of the vampire figure which represents society's fears, reiterated in stories told over hundreds of years. The author situates Dracula's original 'hunting ground' as London, utilising high modality when describing the English as 'endangered by their own modernity, and made vulnerable because of their overconfident belief in rationality and the superiority of race and nation.' This assertion reflects the author's belief in how the original Dracula was born out of England's uncertainty around modernity and cultural ideologies. The article's final paragraph succinctly summarises how 'Dracula, as gothic monster, represents turn-of-the-century fears of immigrants, of modern technology, of Jews, of women's rights, of homosexuality.' This cumulative listing, together with the use of asyndeton, emphasises that these anxieties persist in the 20th century, focusing the reader's attention on how society's anxieties can be reflected through the vampire figure despite centuries separating different vampire stories.*

Multimodal/digital extract 2

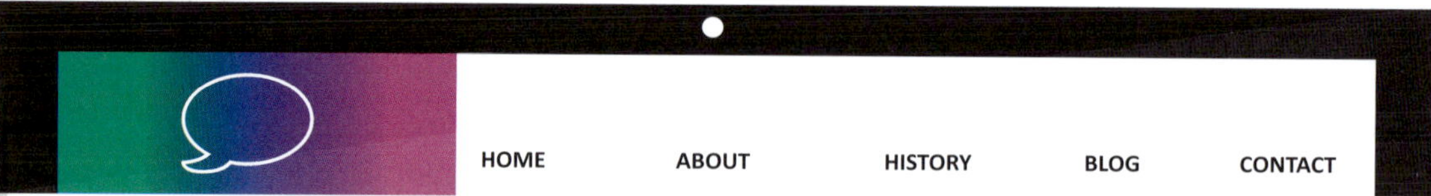

Graphic novels help teens learn about racism, climate change and social justice – here's a reading list

by Karen W Gavigan and Kasey Garrison, *The Conversation*

Teen activists worldwide are making headlines for their social justice advocacy on everything from climate change and immigration to substance abuse and LGBTQ issues. As young people get more vocal about these issues, this trend is being reflected in the graphic novels they are reading.

It's a relatively new genre. The term 'graphic novel' first came about when cartoonist Will Eisner used the phrase to get publishers to recognize his 1978 work, *A Contract with God: And Other Tenement Stories*, as a novel rather than a comic book. Later, to help others understand the term he coined the definition: 'a long comic book that would need a bookmark.'

Later, the cartoonist Art Spiegelman created *Maus*, which relayed his father's experiences during the Holocaust through pictures in which Jews were mice, Germans were cats and Poles were pigs. The book became the first Pulitzer Prize-winning graphic novel in 1992. It was a game-changer, giving credibility to a format that many people, and even Congress, had previously criticized.

Sales have soared since then.

Because the combination of text and images in graphic novels can communicate issues and emotions that words alone often cannot, more educators and parents are finding them to be effective tools for tackling tough issues with kids. The acclaimed author Nikki Giovanni has put it this way. 'A comic book is no longer something to laugh with but something to learn from.'

We are library and information science professors in the US and Australia who are curating a collection of these books to share with educators, parents and students. Here are some highlights, grouped by category.

Racism and other forms of bigotry

In the graphic novel memoir *They Called Us Enemy*, actor, activist and Star Trek legend George Takei partnered with co-authors Justin Eisinger and Steven Scott and the illustrator Harmony Becker to share his family's experience during World War II. During this time, US citizens like Takei's Japanese American family were forcibly moved to internment camps and treated like criminals. Takei encourages readers to give their voices to those who are silenced so that history does not repeat itself.

Another good example in this vein is *New Kid* by African American author and illustrator Jerry Craft. Its main character, Jordan, attends a private school where he is one of the few students of color. Jordan feels like a fish out of water, struggling to fit in at school and his neighborhood. *New Kid* recently won the Newbery Medal – the first time that a graphic novel has won the prestigious US children's literary award.

Excerpt from They Called Us Enemy. Penguin Random House, CC BY-SA

Addiction and mental illness

Jarrett Krosoczka, the author and illustrator of *Hey Kiddo! How I Lost My Mother, Found My Father, and Dealt with Family Addiction*, makes his dysfunctional childhood as normal as possible by expressing himself through drawing. His powerful graphic memoir can help spark discussions about challenging issues with teens.

Another author and illustrator who drew her own path is Katie Green. With stark black-and-white illustrations, she presents the story of her struggle and recovery from eating disorders in *Lighter Than My Shadow*. A scribbly black cloud in the book represents Green's disorders and the anguish that came with them.

Climate change

The graphic anthology *Wild Ocean: Sharks, Whales, Rays, and Other Endangered Sea Creatures* explores the plight and beauty of endangered animals. Overfishing, global warming and other man-made dangers threaten the lives of these sea creatures. This eco-themed book, edited by comic artist and author Matt Dembicki, helps students connect with climate change issues. Reading the book may motivate them to develop ideas to help save our seas.

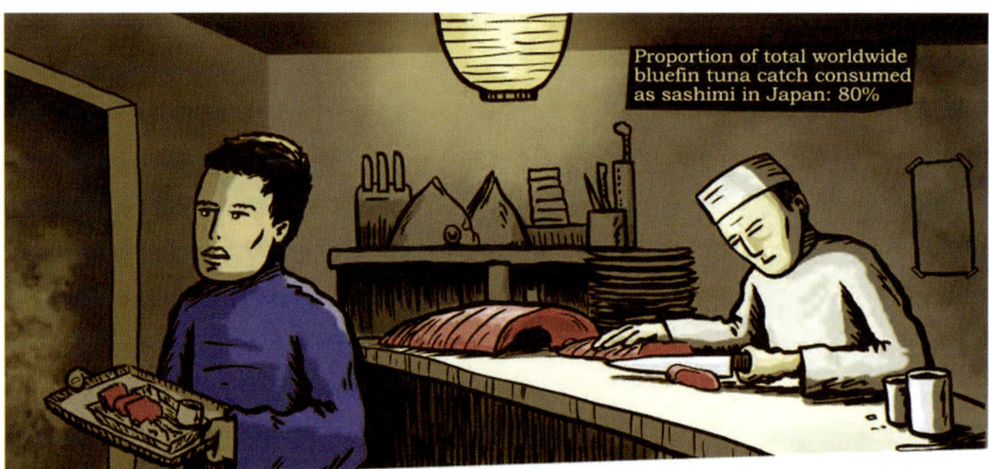

Excerpt from Wild Ocean: Sharks, Whales, Rays, and Other Endangered Sea Creatures. Fulcrum Publishing, CC BY-SA

Immigration and refugees

As the number of worldwide refugees increases, so has the number of graphic novels about them.

Escaping Wars and Waves: Encounters with Syrian Refugees, by the visual journalist Olivier Kugler, *Escape from Syria*, by foreign correspondent Samya Kullab together with illustrator Jackie Roche, and *The Unwanted: Stories of the Syrian*

Refugees, by author and illustrator Don Brown, are powerful stories about Syrians forced to leave their homes and families. Their stories of the refugees' struggles paint a stark picture of a problem that today's young people may well have to fix in the decades ahead.

LGBTQ teens

LGBTQ and intersex teens often feel isolated, confused and afraid while coming to terms with their sexual orientation and gender identity. Reading graphic novels with characters like themselves can help them understand it is OK to be who they are. Likewise, putting a book with these characters in the hands of non-LGBTQ teens can help them empathize with LGBTQ friends.

Bloom, by writer Kevin Panetta and illustrator Savanna Ganucheau, is a graphic novel about Ari, a recent high school graduate. He feels pressured to work in the family bakery rather than following a musical career. When Ari hires a young man as his replacement, love is in the air and ready to bloom.

Answer the following note-taking questions for Multimodal/digital extract 2.

1. Was this composed to inform, persuade or entertain? Who is the audience?

2. What is the subject matter and what components has the composer used to explore it?

3. How is the responder positioned to think and feel by the end of the text?

4. What are the main visual and language techniques? How are they combined/structured to convey meaning?

5. What other significant features or techniques do you notice?

Write a response that answers the following question, using your own notes and the sample response for Multimodal/digital extract 1 as a guide.

Practice question for Multimodal/digital extract 2

Analyse how the article utilises both visual and language features to explore the power of the graphic novel. (4 marks)

Multimodal/digital extract 3

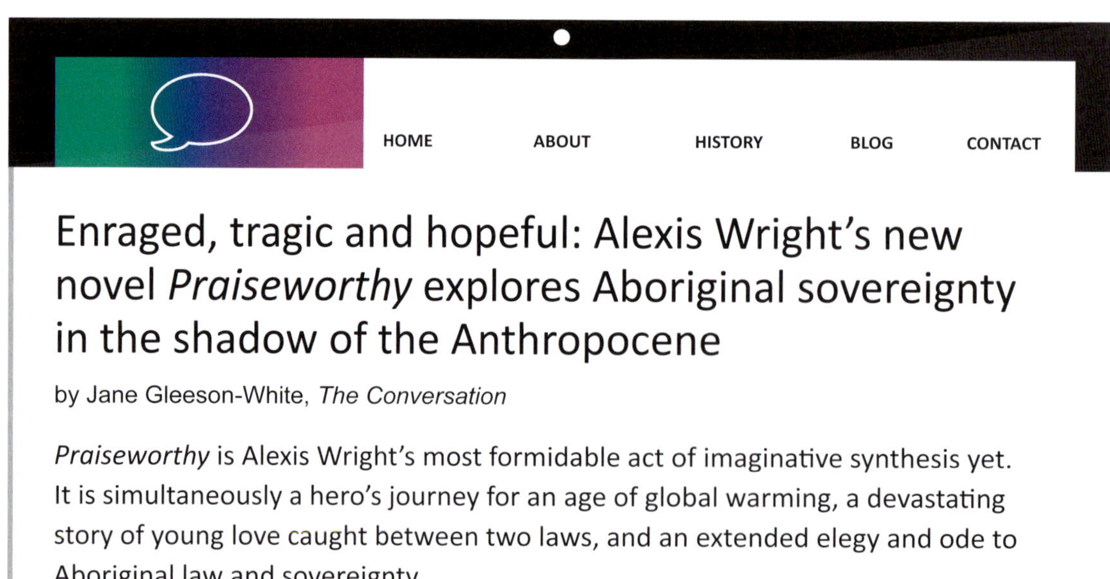

Enraged, tragic and hopeful: Alexis Wright's new novel *Praiseworthy* explores Aboriginal sovereignty in the shadow of the Anthropocene

by Jane Gleeson-White, *The Conversation*

Praiseworthy is Alexis Wright's most formidable act of imaginative synthesis yet. It is simultaneously a hero's journey for an age of global warming, a devastating story of young love caught between two laws, and an extended elegy and ode to Aboriginal law and sovereignty.

It is Wright's most enraged, tragic and hopeful novel to date, with a magnificently upbeat denouement.

In 2019, writing of her storytelling heritage, Wright observed:

> *Even the idea of story is a cultural understanding that story involves all times and realities, the ancient and the new, the story within story within story – all interconnected, all unresolved.*

...

Land theft and its repercussions are invoked on the opening page, where the novel's central character, Cause Man Steel – 'a culture dreamer obsessing about the era' – is introduced alongside the rest of his storm-country people:

> *They knew just as much as he did about surviving on a daily basis, and about how to make sacrifices of themselves in all the cataclysmic times generated by the mangy dogs who had stolen their traditional land.*

But as ever with Wright, before we meet Cause we meet Wright's ancestral Waanyi country, in its cover image inspired by yellow butterflies and its epigraph in the Waanyi language:

> *Kulubibi. Baba yalu kurrkamala, jaja,*
> *(butterflies are flying everywhere)*

Butterflies and their ritual dancing of country are key motifs, associated with the 'moth-er', the story of Aboriginal sovereignty and rebirth.

Vision and ambition

Praiseworthy is Wright's fourth novel and her first since 2013, when her groundbreaking climate-change dystopia *The Swan Book* was published. In the ensuing ten years, the world has changed dramatically – increasingly catastrophic weather events, displacement of peoples and animals, rising inequality, a planetary virus – and yet somehow *The Swan Book* prefigured them all. Such is the force of Wright's literary vision and ambition.

THE MILES FRANKLIN AWARD-WINNING AUTHOR'S TRIBUTE TO THE VISIONARY ABORIGINAL LEADER TRACKER TILMOUTH

In the interim, she wrote *Tracker*, her Stella Prize-winning collective biography of visionary Aboriginal leader and economist Bruce 'Tracker' Tilmouth. Accepting the award in 2018, Wright spoke of the great courage and ambition required to write in these increasingly complex times of multiple crises – and the necessity of doing so.

...

[In *Praiseworthy*,] Cause's thinking is so huge he's called 'Widespread' and 'Planet' by the locals of Praiseworthy, a hot dry town on the Gulf of Carpentaria. His big dream is to make a future for his family and people, independent from the white government. He plans to do this by building a multinational enterprise designed for and profiting from the global climate emergency.

He lives with his wife Dance Steel on their contested Native Title land – the town's graveyard – with their two elusive sons: Tommyhawk, aged eight, and 17-year-old Aboriginal Sovereignty (Ab.Sov for short), so named because these are 'the only words [Cause] loved to say'. Each family member has found a way to hide from the daily horrors of their lives.

...

The two sons learn 'to hide in plain sight by sinking inside themselves'. Glued to his free government digital devices, star student Tommyhawk only communicates through the World Wide Web, which twists his brain into a nightmare of government policy, media whitewashing, and longing to escape to a white heaven called Canberra.

Skinny Aboriginal Sovereignty, who 'has the ancestors dancing in him' like he's the law personified, falls in love with a 15-year-old girl and disappears. Their consummated love is illicit in white Australian law and he pays the price.

An ochre haze

Alexis Wright. Photo: Vincent Long

Cause's plan to bestow his people with 'the gift of infinity' is defiled when 'infinity itself' (Aboriginal Sovereignty) is destroyed. This desecration unleashes an ancestral storm of hate, grief, broken stories, butterfly wings and spirits, which form a huge ochre haze that hovers permanently over Praiseworthy. This sacrilege and its climatic counterpart – the 'Anthropocene haze' – set the story in motion.

...

Evoking Odysseus and the knights of the Holy Grail, Cause is on a quest to find the glistening platinum feral donkey he once saw in a dream. This illusory donkey is destined to be the figurehead of the global transport business that will restore his family fortune: 'their vast traditional lands'.

...

Visionary thinking

... *Praiseworthy* is a novel that creates a literary timespace even more capacious than that of *The Swan Book*.

In the ailing north, far from Canberra, white people barely figure. But their asphyxiating words and thoughts hang over the town like the haze.

...

Sanctity and sacredness

... 'Sixty thousand' is one of the novel's many refrains: lest we forget we are denying justice, equity and respect to the longest surviving First Nations on the planet. *Praiseworthy* suggests that language and stories need to be redefined for these climate-emergency times – and that what is needed is the 'spirit language' of Aboriginal sovereignty, of country: 'The story was always about sanctity, the sacredness of country.'

The novel is Wright's most explicit fictional testament to the time immemorial sovereignty of Aboriginal country, the power of its immutable law and governance, and the almighty eternal presence of its ancestors and spirits, and it attests to the grave danger of disregarding them. There is no ambiguity in this:

> *What couldn't a great ancestor of country do? So, it was exactly like what the old law people had always said would happen if you look after country, country will look after you.*

Or in this:

> *[Aboriginal Sovereignty] had become tied into the chosen shame of a continent stolen from his people by a pack of racists, who had turned the argument against the people whose land they had stolen, and whose intergenerational lives have never recovered from so great a loss..*

The novel's creation has coincided with a global pandemic, lockdowns, continued police violence against Aboriginal men, murders, deaths in custody amid Black Lives Matter marches, and an outpouring of rage against male violence and paedophilia. It illuminates this terrain.

Praiseworthy is a paradox: an epic dirge for the ongoing loss of Aboriginal law and sovereignty – and an ode to the abiding fact that this continent always was and always will be self-governing Aboriginal country. It is creating a new story for these unprecedented times, one capacious enough to contain the feral donkeys that have thrown the old stories into turmoil:

> *Widespread's feral donkeys became complicated plot lines of everything that had ever gone wrong in Praiseworthy from the beginning of colonial oppression, and the symbol of great fallenness, like an ugly fallen angel ...*

Reading this novel reminded me of Samuel Beckett's assessment of James Joyce: 'His writing is not about something. It is the thing itself.' *Praiseworthy* is the thing itself.

Answer the following note-taking questions for Multimodal/digital extract 3.

1. Was this composed to inform, persuade or entertain? Who is the audience?

2. What is the subject matter and what components has the composer used to explore it?

3. How is the responder positioned to think and feel by the end of the text?

4. What are the main visual and language techniques? How are they combined/structured to convey meaning?

5. What other significant features or techniques do you notice?

Write a response that answers the following question, using your own notes and the sample response for Multimodal/digital extract 1 as a guide.

Practice question for Multimodal/digital extract 3

Analyse how the article celebrates the power of storytelling and how it can lead an audience to gain new insights. (5 marks)

Multimodal/digital extract 4

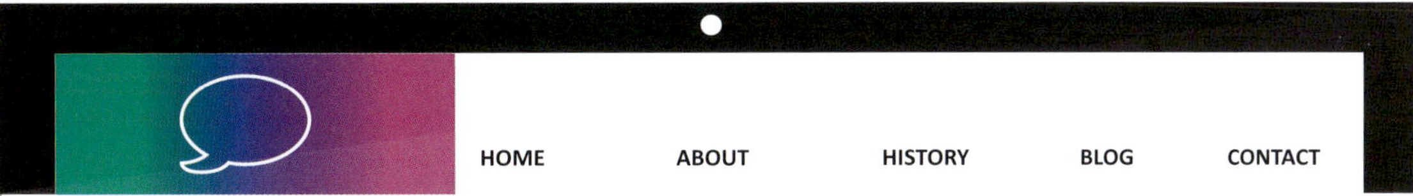

Peace may finally be returning to Yemen, but can a fractured nation be put back together?

by Leena Adel and Ben Rich, *The Conversation*

Last month, China brokered a rapprochement between Saudi Arabia and Iran, a landmark deal that restored full diplomatic ties between the two bitter rivals.

There was hope the detente could also bring an end to one of the world's longest-running – and virtually forgotten – proxy wars in Yemen, as well.

Indeed, peace talks have begun to end the eight years of a brutal conflict between a Saudi-led coalition of nine regional countries and the Iranian-backed Houthi rebels in Yemen. The war has created what is often referred to as the world's worst humanitarian crisis.

Houthi prisoners arrive at the Sana'a airport last week after being released by Saudi Arabia. Hani Mohammed/AP

Despite the exchange of hundreds of prisoners between the adversaries this past week and promising discussions of a permanent ceasefire and the lifting of the Saudi-led blockade of Yemen, however, the path towards peace remains incredibly shaky.

Even more uncertain is whether Yemen can ever recover once the hostilities end.

Yemen in pieces

On my trip to Yemen last July, I (Leena) was stopped by militias at over 40 check-points between the southern city of Aden and the capital, Sana'a. My driver, a doctor before the war, briefed me ahead of each stop regarding the background and affiliates of the checkpoint officers. The brief would change rapidly throughout the 12-hour drive!

On the ground, it was evident the humanitarian crisis had impacted every part of the country and robbed Yemenis of any meaningful prospects. This proxy war, riddled with foreign interests and fuelled by regional and local competition, has left Yemen a fractured nation.

...

The currency used in the south differs from the one in Sana'a. In Aden, the secessionist flag is visible at every turn. In the north, I caught the image of Iranian General Qassem Soleimani, who was assassinated by the US three years ago, hanging in one of the main streets of Sana'a.

Second only to the devastating humanitarian crisis, Yemen's fragmentation is arguably the most detrimental outcome of this war – and the most glaring obstacle to any real solutions to end the crisis.

A member of the Yemeni security personnel inspects a destroyed vehicle in the aftermath of a car bomb attack, which took place a day earlier killing a senior Yemeni military leader along with at least four other people.

Saudi foreign policy moderation

For the Saudis, the peace process appears to be part of a wider trend of foreign policy moderation as the kingdom seeks to retreat from nearly a decade of gaffes, miscalculations and destructive forays abroad.

Since the kingdom's inception in 1932, Saudi diplomacy and security policy have been typified by caution and a desire to maintain the status quo of a regional balance of power.

In this, Riyadh never sought overt domination of the region. It focused its efforts to thwart those who did, such as Egypt under Gamal Abdel Nasser, Iraq under Saddam Hussein and post-revolutionary Iran. Importantly, the Saudis also aimed to avoid direct confrontations, instead utilising their petro wealth and diplomatic influence and alliances when dealing with rivals.

The kingdom's first six monarchs adhered to this approach. But things took a dramatic turn with the ascension of King Salman and the elevation of his heir, Crown Prince Mohammed bin Salman, to key positions in Saudi government in 2015.

Crown Prince Mohammed bin Salman during his meeting with the US president Joe Biden at al-Salman Palace in the Red Sea coastal city of Jeddah on Friday, July 15, 2022. Photo by Saudi press Agency/UPI Credit: UPI/Alamy Live News

Known for his disdain for tradition and self-assured confidence, bin Salman quickly set about defining a new, aggressive foreign policy for the kingdom that eschewed the lessons of the past.

Among other things, this included imposing a blockade on Qatar and only just stopping short of outright invasion, abducting the prime minister of Lebanon, assassinating journalist Jamal Khashoggi and pursuing a provocative approach to its regional rival, Iran.

Under this new muscular foreign policy, the 2015 invasion of Yemen – Saudi Arabia's first-ever major military operation abroad – was intended to be a brief operation that would demonstrate the military and technological prowess of a dynamic and capable kingdom.

...

Eight years on, Riyadh is edging back to a less confrontational posture in the region. After the detente with Iran, resolving the Yemen war would be another important step towards resuming a more 'normal' approach to Saudi foreign policy.

What next for the Yemeni people?

After eight years of bombs, missiles, destruction and hundreds of thousands of civilian deaths, it is the Yemeni people who have lost the most in this war.

...

Finally, peace talks must remain Yemeni-led to eventually pave the path for a Yemeni-led and UN-supported political transition that allows Yemenis to determine the future of their nation.

Answer the following note-taking questions for Multimodal/digital extract 4.

1. Was this composed to inform, persuade or entertain? Who is the audience?

2. What is the subject matter and what components has the composer used to explore it?

3. How is the responder positioned to think and feel by the end of the text?

4. What are the main visual and language techniques? How are they combined/ structured to convey meaning?

5. What other significant features or techniques do you notice?

Write a response that answers the following question, using your own notes and the sample response for Multimodal/digital extract 1 as a guide.

Practice question for Multimodal/digital extract 4

Explain how the article represents the human experience of war. (4 marks)

Multimodal/digital extract 5

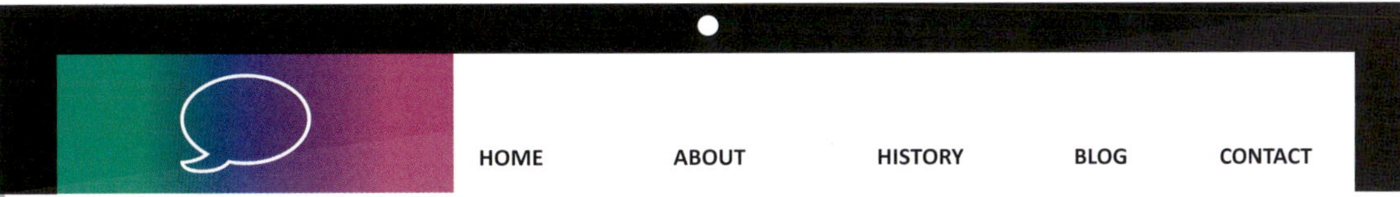

Master your anger – or at least try to understand it

by Nick Haslam, *The Conversation*

Misery is psychology's stale bread and rancid butter. The field heaps attention on sadness, fear and anxiety, and their psychiatric cousins depression, phobia and neurosis.

Anger receives much less scrutiny, but it is a fascinating emotion that is widely misunderstood. People tend to view it as a primitive, irrational, immoral and destructive force – but in many ways it is sophisticated, functional, moral and positive.

Common metaphors reveal a volcanic view of anger. The emotion is often pictured as a hot fluid or gas in a container.

We 'burst', 'fume' or 'well up' with anger. Our blood 'boils'. If it looks as we can't 'contain' our anger we are urged to 'simmer down' or 'blow off steam' rather than 'bottling it up' or 'stewing on it'.

In these metaphors, anger exerts a hot, hydraulic pressure on our capacity for self-control, sometimes exploding out of us.

Indeed, the one mental disorder whose cardinal symptom is seeing red is 'intermittent explosive disorder' – which is pretty much what it sounds like.

Take the pressure down

If we see anger as a dangerous pressure it is no surprise that we think that it is good to release it: better out than in. English poet William Blake said it best:

I was angry with my friend:
I told my wrath, my wrath did end.
I was angry with my foe:
I told it not, my wrath did grow.

This belief in catharsis – the idea that anger should be purged – is largely mistaken.

Expressing anger tends not to relieve the emotion, as the bursting container metaphor would suggest, but instead tends to reinforce and amplify it.

The misconception that anger expressed is anger relieved may contribute to some forms of violence.

There is evidence that playing violent video games increases aggression rather than working it off, and that angry people are drawn to such games because they believe in catharsis.

But research suggests a better way to reduce anger is to reappraise the event that triggered it, reinterpreting it with greater distance and objectivity.

Emotion and morality

The view that anger is hot and primitive also blinds us to the fact it is a moral emotion. To experience anger we must make complex judgements about right and wrong, justice, intention and responsibility.

We feel angry when we think we have been unfairly harmed or that our rights have been violated, and believe that these wrongs have been intentionally inflicted.

In essence, anger is the converse of guilt: the same morally blameworthy acts that make us feel guilt when we commit them against others enrage us when others perpetrate them on us.

People who are quick to anger often see malevolent intentions behind innocuous events, a tendency that resembles paranoia when taken to extremes.

Experimentally-induced anger also boosts the tendency to perceive intentions behind undesirable events. An accidental bump becomes a deliberate slight.

Like paranoiacs, angry people tend to see themselves as righteous victims who have an obligation to give wrongdoers their just deserts.

The positives

The idea of anger as a destructive force also overlooks the fact that anger is in some respects a positive emotion. Although it superficially reflects an unfavourable assessment of the situation, just as sadness and fear reflect perceived loss and threat, anger often feels subjectively positive.

It is not as painful as sadness or fear, and can even be enjoyable, especially when puffed up by righteous indignation.

Anger can also have positive effects. It is an effective fuel for fighting injustice, convincing us of the rightness of our cause, and making our communications more persuasive.

It motivates us to persist in the face of adversity. It can – up to a point – improve outcomes in negotiation by drawing concessions from others.

It can reduce pain, especially with the aid of energetic cursing. It can make us more creative.

Anger is also an at least partially positive emotion at the level of the brain.

It shares with other positive emotions such as happiness a pattern of selective activation in the left hemisphere, whereas negative emotions typically activate more on the right.

The neural circuitry underpinning it drives approach behaviour rather than the avoidance behaviour common to negative emotions such as sadness and fear.

When we are angry we move towards whatever it is that challenges us, just as we move towards things we like and enjoy when we are happy.

Of course, anger can be destructive. It can spark violence and disproportionate revenge. It makes us worse drivers.

Angry rumination – brooding – taxes our body's stress response and increases the tendency for intoxicated people to behave aggressively.

Anger tends to be self-serving and egocentric, triggered selectively when bad things impinge on us but not when they harm others. But it is not a mindless primitive instinct or a boiling emotional magma.

If we could understand this better we might get beyond the view that anger should be released in a rush of blood and find ways to regulate, restrain and master it instead.

Answer the following note-taking questions for Multimodal/digital extract 5.

1. Was this composed to inform, persuade or entertain? Who is the audience?

2. What is the subject matter and what components has the composer used to explore it?

3. How is the responder positioned to think and feel by the end of the text?

4. What are the main visual and language techniques? How are they combined/structured to convey meaning?

5. What other significant features or techniques do you notice?

Write a response that answers the following question, using your own notes and the sample response for Multimodal/digital extract 1 as a guide.

Practice question for Multimodal/digital extract 5

Critically analyse how the author uses the language within the text to capture the complexity of anger. (5 marks)

Multimodal/digital extract 6

Does Australia 'get' culture?

by Julian Meyrick, *The Conversation*

Why doesn't Australia *get* culture? What is it about culture that defeats our perception to the point where, like an unwelcome magic trick, it vanishes as an object of collective concern?

For a country so settled it has no dialects and doesn't bother with a national bill of rights, what is it about culture – the normal accompaniment of national cohesion – we fail to discern and value? Why does the nasally satire of Monty Python's 'Bruces' sketch still bite, 43 years after it was first broadcast?

Why, after all the attention, achievement and acclamation our cultural sector has garnered, when it has ballooned in size and financial contribution, when it is part of every moment of our complex waking lives, is it often regarded as little better, in the inimitable words of Barry Humphries' character Sandy Stone, than a very nice night's entertainment?

...

All Australians

Today, culture matters more than ever. The 19th century was the age of mass military mobilisation, the 20th of mass economic mobilisation. The 21st century is the age of mass cultural mobilisation, and beyond the immersive hedonism of our shopping malls and the art-free minds of many of our politicians, collisions rage between whole ways of life in which culture is the content, framework and bloody inspiration.

However dysfunctional such polities may be, they are aware in a way that we are not of the centrality of culture, its capacity to be both limitlessly diverse and powerfully binding. We are not all rich. We are not all white. But we are all Australians, of one kind or another.

Indigenous artist Lena Nyadbi. Alan Porritt/AAP

That should mean more than footy loyalties and welling up with tears on Anzac Day. It should mean an internal order of value that allows us to articulate who we are and engage with those who are not as we are.

A national culture is not the opposite of cosmopolitan awareness. It is its ground and guarantee. Without a grasp of the importance of our own culture how can we appreciate anyone else's?

Mrs Edna Everage.

The accident of English

There are two reasons why Australia's sense of a national culture is weak and intermittent. The first is to do with language. The accident of English allows us to free-ride the cultural goods and services of the two international powers that have so far dominated our fate, Britain and the US.

Our quest for independence did not involve the assertion of a separate linguistic identity, as with Israel, or a contested one, such as bilingual Canada. Uniquely among post-colonial countries we do not have a national theatre. Instead, we are a net cultural importer, soaking up the art developed for other people and sensibilities.

I grew up the son of a (very) English father and a (trenchantly) Australian mother, the recipient of two different ways of looking at culture that don't meet on equal terms. The Anglo-Saxon countries cast a long shadow, supplying us not only with cultural objects and experiences but with expectations too.

As Australian writer AA Phillips famously put it in 1950:

> *In the back of the Australian mind, there sits a minatory Englishman … Subconsciously the educated Australian feels a guilty need to placate this shadowy figure.*

This ascendancy has lessened over the years but has it gone away? Watching the Australian film industry wither on the vine, our television drama go from worse to worser, and our theatre gorge itself on foreign classics, it's tempting to think not.

The second reason has to do with our peaceful history. No major wars have been fought on Australian soil (or none that we openly acknowledge, at any rate). Our cultural consciousness has never been pushed into sharp awareness by invasion or forced colonisation.

Geoffrey Blainey's *The Tyranny of Distance* has allowed a feeling of unthreatened relaxation that has bordered on inertia. Culture touches everyone's life. But because no-one has ever tried to take ours away, it remains under-served.

Unless you are Indigenous, of course, in which case you will be acutely aware that in the modern, mobilised world, politics and culture are the same side of the one coin.

Turning away

... After 1945, Europe and America started promoting their own culture, getting serious about it once they realised that's where most people live their lives.

Increased leisure time, the egalitarianism war's sacrifices brought, and a new interest in cultural activities of all kinds, led to arts councils, touring programs, cultural exchange.

Looking at the sorry mess of the Middle East and Afghanistan today you feel that's a lesson the West needs to learn all over again.

Australia never learnt it. We took an opposite tack, erecting a barrier designed to keep the rest of the world out – the White Australia policy. In turning away from the world, we turned away from ourselves. The cultural history of Australia in the 1950s and 1960s is depressing not because so little happened but because so much tried to.

As good as it gets

Australia is now one of the most privileged countries in the richest epoch in the whole of human history. Economically, it doesn't get much better. Yet the last election was fought in a flailing panic of gratuitous materialism and widespread whinging about standards of living.

Journalist Tom Allard noted 'the disconnect between reality and sentiment'. Meanwhile, economist Professor Ross Garnaut warned of:

> *a new political culture that elevates private over public interests and the immediate over the longer term. If we continue within the political culture ... we will live in greater comfort for a short while. But sooner rather than later we will experience deep economic recession with high unemployment. We can expect bitter conflict within our society, and unhappiness about our institutions.*

A sense of culture

We are a country not without culture but without a sense of culture. That distinction is crucial. Australia does not lack art, artists or audiences. But as a nation we find it hard to see culture in any but consumerist terms.

...

Launching Sophia Turkiewicz's *Once My Mother* in August, for example, Australian director Robert Connolly delivered a withering assessment of the current state of documentary film financing.

Turkiewicz starting looking for support in 1975 – which makes her hardihood notable even by Australian standards. Long-form documentaries fall between the cracks of current production models. That this is more than a glitch is evidenced by the fact documentary film-making is fast migrating to the internet, where interactive, multi-platform formats offer greater diversity and creative sophistication.

In 2011, *Once My Mother* finally attracted support from Screen Australia's Signature Documentary Program, a fund established in 2011 aimed at documentary storytelling that is bold in form and content.

…

Stories of systemic frustration can be found in every area of Australian culture, both the traditional high arts and the newer creative industries. They indicate a situation whereby commercial imperatives block artistic ones because the internal order of value that should keep them in productive tension is not present to the needed degree.

Due process

So where do we go from here? Fortunately, Australia's weak sense of culture has produced a compensating strength: its cultural policy process.

…

Labor and Liberal governments have both contributed to developing cultural policy as a positive field of endeavour. Given that the bureaucratic provision of something as wayward as culture is difficult to begin with, Australia has done well in utilising its support infrastructure (the Australia Council is going strong 15 years after the UK replaced its own independent Arts Council with a hands-on Ministry of culture which, surprise, surprise, doesn't work any better).

…

Culture warrants a high position in the new government's pecking order. If Australia is to *get* culture any time soon, it will need leadership from the centre. The administrative machinery and money are there (despite our complaints).

What's needed is an evolved policy vision.

Answer the following note-taking questions for Multimodal/ digital extract 6.

1. Was this composed to inform, persuade or entertain? Who is the audience?

____

____

2. What is the subject matter and what components has the composer used to explore it?

____

____

3. How is the responder positioned to think and feel by the end of the text?

____

____

4. What are the main visual and language techniques? How are they combined/ structured to convey meaning?

____

____

5. What other significant features or techniques do you notice?

____

____

Write a response that answers the following question, using your own notes and the sample response for Multimodal/digital extract 1 as a guide.

Practice question for Multimodal/digital extract 6

Does the article explore the paradox of Australians 'getting' culture? Discuss. (5 marks)

____

____

____

____

____

____

____

____

____

____

Using your notes for Multimodal/digital extracts 4 and 6, write a response that answers the following comparative question. Remember that you can reuse your previous quotes and techniques. Note that this question is worth 6 marks, requiring the balanced comparison of the two texts and substantial textual evidence from both extracts to support your answer.

Comparative question – Multimodal/digital extracts 4 and 6

Compare how Multimodal/digital extracts 4 and 6 represent the responsibility of those in power to create change. (6 marks)

HINTS:

Consider what is being changed or is remaining unchanged in both texts.

Consider the tone of the authors – how do they depict those in power?

7 CHAPTER

Practice questions

In this chapter you will cover:

- how to deconstruct a question
- bands in marking criteria – low, middle and top
- rewriting activities
- checklist for self-editing and improvement
- practice examinations
- useful words to use in your responses.

How to deconstruct a question

Step 1 Identify the key words from the question

A good starting point when identifying the keywords is to look at the verbs and nouns in the question. The *verbs* relate to what you must do and the *nouns* relate to what you must identify clearly.

In the table below are some of the sample questions from Chapters 2–6 of this book. Highlight the verbs and nouns in these sample questions.

Fiction	Explain how the fiction extract explores how introspection can lead an individual to a greater understanding of the world. (5 marks)
Nonfiction	Analyse how the author has used language to highlight the dangerous experiences that can occur when travelling. (4 marks)
Visual text	How does the image convey ideas about reading? (3 marks)
Poetry	How does the poem explore the impact of loss? (4 marks)
Multimodal/ digital text	How does the article highlight the power of storytelling in capturing particular cultures across time? (4 marks)

Other verbs used in short answer questions could include:

- *Compare* (this verb means you should look for both similarities and differences between two things. Examples of these things include similar or contrasting ideas from different texts, different perspectives within a single text or different language features within the same text/between different texts)
- *Contrast* (this verb means you must note differences between two things)
- *Reflect* (this verb is not as common, but when 'reflect on' is used, it often means you will need to draw upon the intended reader's or composer's understanding and/or assumptions and perhaps express how the text has affected your thinking about something)
- *Evaluate* (this verb is used for longer responses which can also often be comparative. 'Evaluate' is a higher order critical verb, which is why it is often reserved for essay questions. It requires you to make judgements about texts and the effectiveness of the language and features used within them.)

Step 2 Identify the parts of the question

Identifying how many different parts there are in a question is important when there are *multiple nouns* which depend on one another.

For example, in the Multimodal/digital question in the table, the question asks how the article highlights the *power of storytelling* in capturing *particular cultures across time*. If a student identifies ideas about different cultures in different times, but does not analyse what the article says about the power of storytelling in relation to these cultures, they will not be able to achieve a top range mark because they have not addressed the entire question.

Deconstructing questions: practice task

The following questions are written in the style of HSC English examination questions. Deconstruct them by:

- identifying the verb(s)
- identifying the noun(s)
- identifying how many parts there are to the question.

Text 1 — Prose fiction extract (4 marks) **Analyse how the writer represents the feeling of freedom in this extract.**	Verb(s): Noun(s): Parts:
Text 2 — Feature article extract (5 marks) **In what ways do the language and images convey the effect that hindsight can have?**	Verb(s): Noun(s): Parts:
Text 3 — Poem (3 marks) **In what ways does the poet celebrate inclusivity?**	Verb(s): Noun(s): Parts:
Text 4 — Prose fiction extract (4 marks) **Analyse how the writer captures the narrator's experience of heartbreak and regret.**	Verb(s): Noun(s): Parts:
Text 5 — Interview extract (4 marks) **Explain how the interviewer explores the paradoxes of human behaviour in this extract.**	Verb(s): Noun(s): Parts:

Bands in marking criteria – low, middle and top

The marking criteria in Section I of Paper 1 in the HSC English examination have between 3 and 5 bands.

Sometimes, each mark value will have its own band, like this:

CRITERIA	MARKS
Explains effectively how [name of text] encourages us to appreciate the past using detailed, well-chosen supporting evidence	4
Explains how [name of text] encourages us to appreciate the past using some supporting evidence	3
Describes how [name of text] encourages us to appreciate the past	2
Makes some relevant points about [name of text]	1

Other times, some bands will have more than one mark value, like this:

CRITERIA	MARKS
Explains effectively how [name of text] explores the healing power of nature using detailed, well-chosen supporting evidence	6
Explains how [name of text] explores the healing power of nature using well-chosen supporting evidence	4–5
Describes how [name of text] explores the healing power of nature using some supporting evidence	2–3
Makes relevant points about the healing power of nature in [name of text]	1

In order to achieve the top band of the marking criteria and avoid being in the middle or low band, you must ensure that you are analysing your text in sufficient detail. You need to avoid simply describing the text or listing techniques and features of the text which have no relevance to the question.

When you are describing, you only need to name and identify the object of the description and then identify some features and characteristics.

When you are analysing, you must name and identify what you will be analysing, identify some features/characteristics, write about the effect of these characteristics and connect relevant examples to the question.

DESCRIBE	ANALYSE
Identify the human experience/technique	Identify what the key terms from the question are in the text you are examining – i.e. the human experience in this text AND/OR Identify the technique if the question is a technique-driven question
Describe the features of the text	Describe the features of the text using quotes and specific references
	Use 'cause and effect' language/verbs in your analysis – relate the effect of the techniques to the human experience you identified in your topic sentence Analyse the effect of the technique and how this connects to the question

Below is a sample of a low range response. It is a low range response because it shows some understanding of the text, but it does not connect this understanding to clear quotes or techniques.

Text 1 — Prose fiction extract (4 marks)

Analyse how the writer represents the feeling of freedom.

In the prose fiction extract, they are looking at the ocean and thinking about their life. The extract describes a man lying on the deck of the boat while he has a drink. It is sunny which makes the man feel happy and the writer uses sensory language to help draw the reader into the text and convey the writer's intention.

Below is a sample of a middle range response. It is a middle range response because it is *describing* the text instead of *analysing* the text.

Text 1 — Prose fiction extract (4 marks)

Analyse how the writer represents the feeling of freedom.

In the prose fiction extract, the protagonist is travelling on a boat. Listing is used in the quote 'lying on the deck, sipping a drink, blinking lazily in the sunlight.' This helps the author convey what the boat journey is like. Sensory language helps to make the experience seem positive through 'the warm, salty air of the ocean buffeting his face' which helps capture the air rushing past the ship.

Now look at this example, which *analyses* the text instead of *describing* it.

Text 1 — Prose fiction extract (4 marks)

Analyse how the writer represents the feeling of freedom.

In the prose fiction extract the protagonist experiences feeling free through travelling on a boat and leaving his everyday troubles. Listing is used in the quote 'lying on the deck, sipping a drink, blinking lazily in the sunlight' which conveys how the protagonist has the freedom to do what he likes during the boat journey. Sensory language describing 'the warm, salty air of the ocean buffeting his face' helps to capture the feeling of liberation the protagonist feels as he looks back at the shore while the boat leaves.

The following is a sample set of marking criteria for the 4 mark question above. Take note of the underlined verbs (and adverb), and how these decrease in complexity to indicate the depth of analysis.

CRITERIA	MARKS
<u>Analyses effectively</u> how the writer represents the feeling of freedom using well-chosen supporting evidence	4
<u>Analyses</u> how the writer represents the feeling of freedom using some supporting evidence	3
<u>Explains</u> how the writer represents the feeling of freedom	2
<u>Provides</u> some relevant information about the text	1

Rewriting activities

Low and middle range sample responses for some of the practice questions and sample texts in chapters 2–6 are included in this section.

Review the marking criteria, sample responses from the previous chapters and the advice from this chapter, then use these to help you rewrite the responses to ensure they score in the top band.

Low–middle range sample response: Fiction

(See page 15 for the sample Fiction text and response.)

FICTION	**Explain how the fiction extract explores how introspection can lead an individual to a greater understanding of the world. (5 marks)**

Read this sample response and get ready to rewrite it.

The narrator is thinking about their lifestyle with the composer utilising sensory language, listing, past tense and dialogue to convey their point. The narrator de-

scribes the weather 'it was a warm season, and I had just left a country of wide lawns and friendly trees', utilising sensory language and personification to make the city seem inviting. This helps the reader understand that the world is a nice place. When the narrator reflects on the war experience a simile is used 'the Middle West now seemed like the ragged edge of the universe'. This simile helps the reader understand how the narrator feels and this leads them to a greater understanding of the world.

First, write down your notes on how this response can be improved. Use the checklist for self-editing and improvement on page 150 to help you.

- Is this a low or middle range response? What makes you think that?
- Structure – does it have a topic sentence and clear flow of analysis?
- Length – is it the correct length for the mark value?
- Techniques and quotes – are these correct and relevant?
- Grammar and syntax – are there any errors which affect the clarity of expression?

Now rewrite the response in the box below.

Low–middle range sample response: Nonfiction

(See page 42 for the sample Nonfiction text and response.)

NONFICTION	**Analyse how the author has used language to highlight the dangerous experiences that can occur when travelling. (4 marks)**

Read this sample response and get ready to rewrite it.

The author has used the English language to show how dangerous Australian tourists are. This is because they are reckless people who don't think about what they're doing. The title 'Fatal attraction' shows how dangerous and attractive Australians are which can be bad for anybody meeting up with them. They die a lot 'as a result of misadventure, are victims of robbery and are on drugs.'

First, write down your notes on how this response can be improved. Use the checklist for self-editing and improvement on page 150 to help you.

- Is this a low or middle range response? What makes you think that?
- Structure – does it have a topic sentence and clear flow of analysis?
- Length – is it the correct length for the mark value?
- Techniques and quotes – are these correct and relevant?
- Grammar and syntax – are there any errors which affect the clarity of expression?

Now rewrite the response in the box below.

Low–middle range sample response: Visual text

(See page 68 for the sample Visual text and response.)

VISUALS **How does the image convey ideas about reading? (3 marks)**

Read this sample response and get ready to rewrite it.

Reading is an important part of the human experience which can help us understand particular lives and cultures. Different colours are used to convey the joy that comes from reading which burst from the book and draw my eyes to the key feature – the book.

First, write down your notes on how this response can be improved. Use the checklist for self-editing and improvement on page 150 to help you.

- Is this a low or middle range response? What makes you think that?
- Structure – does it have a topic sentence and clear flow of analysis?
- Length – is it the correct length for the mark value?
- Techniques and quotes – are these correct and relevant?
- Grammar and syntax – are there any errors which affect the clarity of expression?

Now rewrite the response in the box below.

Low–middle range sample response: Poetry

(See page 85 for the sample Poetry text and response.)

POETRY	How does the poem explore the impact of loss? (4 marks)

Read this sample response and get ready to rewrite it.

This poem is about missing what you've lost like memories of living on a hill by a river. The emotions evoked are sadness, happiness, joy and regret. The places are a hill, an old summerhouse and the banks of a river. There is sensory language in the quote 'hills of blue,/Blind drifts of vapour blow,' which helps draw out the emotions. The diction of 'gaunt trees that interlace' helps the reader understand that the trees are old and sick looking.

First, write down your notes on how this response can be improved. Use the checklist for self-editing and improvement on page 150 to help you.

- Is this a low or middle range response? What makes you think that?
- Structure – does it have a topic sentence and clear flow of analysis?
- Length – is it the correct length for the mark value?
- Techniques and quotes – are these correct and relevant?
- Grammar and syntax – are there any errors which affect the clarity of expression?

Now rewrite the response in the box below.

Low–middle range sample response: Multimodal/digital text

(See page 110 for the sample Multimodal/digital text and response.)

MULTIMODAL/ DIGITAL	**How does the article highlight the power of storytelling in capturing particular cultures across time? (4 marks)**

Read this sample response and get ready to rewrite it.

> *Across time vampires have been made into stories because they scare people constantly and people seem to like stories about vampires because* Dracula *and* Interviews with a Vampire *and books like* Twilight *keep getting made into shows and books. These are mainly teenage girl cultures who like these stories which gives insight into what popular girl culture like to read about. The article uses a lot of red and black in the images because these symbolise blood, murder, sex and evil which is what the vampire culture is all about. The vampire also represented moral contamination and liberated new women as well as homosexuality. This makes Dracula's monstrosity threaten to uncover the frailty of Britain's imperial mastery and – as with Harker – its masculinity.*

First, write down your notes on how this response can be improved. Use the checklist for self-editing and improvement on page 150 to help you.

- Is this a low or middle range response? What makes you think that?
- Structure – does it have a topic sentence and clear flow of analysis?
- Length – is it the correct length for the mark value?
- Techniques and quotes – are these correct and relevant?
- Grammar and syntax – are there any errors which affect the clarity of expression?

Now rewrite the response in the box below.

Checklist for self-editing and improvement

Use the checklist below to review your practice responses.

What, how and why

The WHAT:

- ☐ Have you used the key term(s) from the question in your topic sentence (or mini-thesis if it's a comparative question)?
- ☐ Have you answered the question by clearly identifying WHAT each key term in the question is within the text you are analysing?
- ☐ Did you address all the parts of the question in your topic sentence?
- ☐ Have you avoided simply listing techniques in the first sentence *unless* the question specifically asks for techniques?

Note the four points above. This is the most crucial part of your response, where you prove that you understand the text and that you are answering the question, not just listing techniques.

Many of the responses that end up in the middle range will use the key terms from the question without clearly proving they have comprehended what the text is actually about.

The HOW:

- ☐ Have you clearly identified a correct example/quote containing a relevant technique(s)?
- ☐ Have you clearly identified the technique(s)?
- ☐ Have you included the right amount of textual evidence which matches the mark value of the question?

The WHY:

- ☐ Have you analysed the effect of the technique(s)?
- ☐ Have you analysed the effect of the technique(s) and written about their significance in relation to your topic sentence?

Note the difference between the two points above. This is another pitfall to avoid, as some students can default into listing analysis of various techniques but not actually address the question.

- ☐ Have you expanded upon a specific aspect of the text/topic sentence within this analysis? (If you repeat the same idea/phrase from your topic sentence, this can give your marker the impression that you only have a superficial understanding of the text.)
- ☐ Does your analysis prove that you understand what is happening in the text?

Expression, structure and analysis

- ☐ Are there any lapses in grammar that affect the clarity of your ideas?
- ☐ Is your response structured appropriately for the mark value?
- ☐ Does it follow a clear structure (PEEL/PETA, etc.) so the marker can discern the WHAT, HOW and WHY?
- ☐ Does it have paragraphs if it is a comparative question/high mark value question?
- ☐ Is it the appropriate length for the mark value?
- ☐ Have you been concise in your phrasing to avoid 'filler phrases' which eat up your word limit and time?
- ☐ Have you included unnecessary extra terms from the Common Module: Texts and Human Experiences rubric in your response (which are not asked for in this question)?
- ☐ What is the ratio of quotes/textual reference to analysis? Are the quotes too long, or is there too much description of the text and not enough of your own analysis?

e.g. The COMPOSER of TEXT 1 made NAME OF TEXT to convey that ALL THE TERMS IN THE QUESTION which is shown through LIST OF TECHNIQUES which helps responders understand LIST OF RUBRIC TERMS.

Choose the specific terms and ideas which directly address the question you have been asked. Don't include filler words, rubric terms and lists of techniques that you don't need. You are not expected to analyse the entire text or write about the entire human experience. Be selective and structure your response clearly according to the question to ensure that you are engaging in analysis that is relevant to the question and demonstrates your understanding of the text.

A useful self-review activity is to highlight sections of your analysis to ensure you have *analysed* your text instead of just *describing* it. You will need four colours and some of your own practice responses for this activity.

Connect to the question	Analyse the effect of the technique and how this connects to the question
Analyse 'cause and effect' of the characteristics	Use 'cause and effect' language/verbs in your analysis – relate the effect of the techniques to the human experience you identified in your topic sentence
Describe features and characteristics	Describe the specific features or characteristics of the text using quotes and specific references
Name and identify	Identify what the key terms from the question are in the text you are examining – i.e. the human experience in this text. AND/OR Identify the technique if the question is a technique-driven question

After completing the following practice examinations, you should complete the highlighting activity above, applying it to your responses.

INSIGHT PUBLICATIONS PRACTICE HIGHER SCHOOL CERTIFICATE EXAMINATION

English Standard/Advanced

Paper 1 – Texts and Human Experiences

Stimulus Booklet

Notes:

1. *This practice examination can be completed by students of both English Standard and English Advanced. In the Higher School Certificate examination, there will be two different papers: you will complete either the Standard paper or the Advanced paper.*

2. *You will receive two separate booklets for the examination. One is the Stimulus Booklet containing all the unseen texts, and the other is the booklet containing all the questions, where you will write your answers for Section I.*

Section I

Text 1 — Prose fiction extract

I was born in the year 18— to a large fortune, endowed besides with excellent parts, inclined by nature to industry, fond of the respect of the wise and good among my fellowmen, and thus, as might have been supposed, with every guarantee of an honourable and distinguished future. And indeed the worst of my faults was a certain impatient gaiety of disposition, such as has made the happiness of many, but such as I found it hard to reconcile with my imperious desire to carry my head high, and wear a more than commonly grave countenance before the public. Hence it came about that I concealed my pleasures; and that when I reached years of reflection, and began to look round me and take stock of my progress and position in the world, I stood already committed to a profound duplicity of life. Many a man would have even blazoned such irregularities as I was guilty of; but from the high views that I had set before me, I regarded and hid them with an almost morbid sense of shame. It was thus rather the exacting nature of my aspirations than any particular degradation in my faults, that made me what I was, and, with even a deeper trench than in the majority of men, severed in me those provinces of good and ill which divide and compound man's dual nature. In this case, I was driven to reflect deeply and inveterately on that hard law of life, which lies at the root of religion and is one of the most plentiful springs of distress. Though so profound a double-dealer, I was in no sense a hypocrite; both sides of me were in dead earnest; I was no more myself when I laid aside restraint and plunged in shame, than when I laboured, in the eye of day, at the furtherance of knowledge or the relief of sorrow and suffering. And it chanced that the direction of my scientific studies, which led wholly towards the mystic and the transcendental, reacted and shed a strong light on this consciousness of the perennial war among my members. With every day, and from both sides of my intelligence, the moral and the intellectual, I thus drew steadily nearer to that truth, by whose partial discovery I have been doomed to such a dreadful shipwreck: that man is not truly one, but truly two. I say two, because the state of my own knowledge does not pass beyond that point. Others will follow, others will outstrip me on the same lines; and I hazard the guess that man will be ultimately known for a mere polity of multifarious, incongruous and independent denizens. I, for my part, from the nature of my life, advanced infallibly in one direction and in one direction only. It was on the moral side, and in my own person, that I learned to recognise the thorough and primitive duality of man; I saw that, of the two natures that contended in the field of my consciousness, even if I could rightly be said to be either, it was only because I was radically both; and from an early date, even before the course of my scientific discoveries had begun to suggest the most naked possibility of such a miracle, I had learned to dwell with pleasure, as a beloved daydream, on the thought of the separation of these elements. If each, I told myself, could be housed in separate identities, life would be relieved of all that was unbearable; the unjust might go his way, delivered from the aspirations and remorse of his more upright twin; and the just could walk steadfastly and securely on his upward path, doing the good things in which he found his pleasure, and no longer exposed to disgrace and penitence by the hands of this extraneous evil.

...

The most racking pangs succeeded: a grinding in the bones, deadly nausea, and a horror of the spirit that cannot be exceeded at the hour of birth or death. Then these agonies began swiftly to subside, and I came to myself as if out of a great sickness. There was something strange in my sensations, something indescribably new and, from its very novelty, incredibly sweet. I felt younger, lighter, happier in body; within I was conscious of a heady recklessness, a current of disordered sensual images running like a millrace in my fancy, a solution of the bonds of obligation, an unknown but not an innocent freedom of the soul. I knew myself, at the first breath of this new life, to be more wicked, tenfold more wicked, sold a slave to my original evil; and the thought, in that moment, braced and delighted me like wine. I stretched out my hands, exulting in the freshness of these sensations; and in the act, I was suddenly aware that I had lost in stature.

There was no mirror, at that date, in my room; that which stands beside me as I write, was brought there later on and for the very purpose of these transformations. The night however, was far gone into the morning – the morning, black as it was, was nearly ripe for the conception of the day – the inmates of my house were locked in the most rigorous hours of slumber; and I determined, flushed as I was with hope and triumph, to venture in my new shape as far as to my bedroom. I crossed the yard, wherein the constellations looked down upon me, I could have thought, with wonder, the first creature of that sort that their unsleeping vigilance had yet disclosed to them; I stole through the corridors, a stranger in my own house; and coming to my room, I saw for the first time the appearance of Edward Hyde.

Robert Louis Stevenson
Extract from Strange Case of Dr Jekyll and Mr Hyde

End of Text 1

Text 2 — Visual text

End of Text 2

Text 3 — Feature article extract

CAN DEATH ON THE SCREEN FEEL THE SAME AS A 'REAL' ONE?

Death is a part of life, an adage usually reserved for those who physically exist in our lives – family, friends, colleagues, acquaintances. So what happens when a profound death experience happens on the screen? Is that still a legitimate experience of mourning?

This week, the popular TV show *Succession* had a significant 'on screen' death – where even the cast filming the scene spoke as if the response to the trauma had a very real feeling.

In the same way as the cast, social media reactions to the sudden and unexpected death of a person with a complex character, after four seasons of growing to understand them, can feel like the death of someone you actually know.

The research behind this phenomenon can be found as far back as the 1970s when early understandings around the death of a main character on children's television served to provide real world insight into the irreversibility of death as a universal experience.

Over time, as popular culture and television became more nuanced, the diversity of the ways in which death occurred in fictional programs began to replicate the complexity of 'real' loss in our lives. Via television, we get access to catastrophic loss, multiple casualty events, loss after significant illness – as well as seeing how death impacts the people left behind.

In the most recent episode of *Succession*, we also see what happens when a death occurs involving a person where their character or relationship to others is strained. We see ways in which grief is not always a by-product of love.

Why does this grief feel real from an armchair perspective?

Death on screen can also act as a trigger or a reminder of the losses we have endured.

When a show realistically portrays grief in its purest form, the emotive or reflective reaction can unlock our own grief. Engaging with the small screen is an overt act of escapism, often for entertainment. We might be switching on a program with the intention of relaxation, only to be met with trauma and sadness.

When a sudden loss is brought into our lounge rooms, or via the devices on our laps, we experience shock, confusion and anger about the abruptness of an event, just like the feelings we can experience when loss happens suddenly in our real lives.

Safe reporting of sudden and traumatic death on fictional TV shows is not covered by media reporting guidelines. Warnings prior to a scene, or consistent information at the end of an episode about seeking additional support, might be minimal.

Recent research identifies multiple contexts related to warnings where TV shows may note that an episode will explore death, however, the complexity of how this might be portrayed is limited.

What is this grief called?

While there is no rulebook for grief, reacting emotionally to a small screen death can bring about concerns that we look silly or that we lack awareness of the distinction between reality and fiction. This form of parasocial grieving, described as having feelings attached to a pseudo-relationship, does feel real, does have consequences and does need space to be managed.

We don't all watch the same shows, we don't all respond to the death of a character the same way, we might even struggle to understand why people have the reactions they do when a TV death occurs. I would encourage you to pause for a moment and remember the ones that did get under our skin.

In 1985, Australian viewers lived through the death of Molly from *A Country Practice*, where the final image of a mother's end-stage cancer diagnosis played out while watching her daughter fly a kite.

Teens watching Sarah Michelle Gellar stumble across the sudden untimely death of her mother in *Buffy the Vampire Slayer* shaped many feelings when there is a catastrophic loss without warning.

In the last decade, the sudden death of Patrick from *Offspring* had people legitimately calling in sick from work the next day.

The global reaction to the Red Wedding scene in *Game of Thrones* had forums on Reddit unpacking why so many characters were murdered and sharing the impact of the sights and sounds of blood and murder and traumatic grief.

We engage in a social contract when we connect to a TV show. We expect to be removed from our real life and engage in the viewing of other spaces. Death in those spaces – and the reactions to that loss – can feel as if they break that contract.

Sarah Wayland
Extract from 'Can death on the screen feel the same as a "real" one?'
The Conversation
theconversation.com/can-death-on-the-screen-feel-the-same-as-a-real-one-203549

End of Text 3

Text 4 — Poem

WHERE I AM NOT

I ask the new migrant if he regrets leaving Russia.
We have dispensed already with my ancestry.
He says no. For a time, he was depressed. He found
with every return he missed what he left behind.
A constant state of this. Better to love by far
where you are. He taps the steering wheel of his car,
the hum of the engine an imperceptible tremble
in us. When he isn't driving, he works tending
to new trees. I've seen these saplings popping
up all over the suburbs, tickling the bellies
of bridges, the new rooted darlings of the State.
The council spent a quarter mil on them &
someone, he – Lilian – must ensure the dirt
holds. Gentrification is climate-friendly now.
I laugh and he laughs, and we eat the distance
between histories. He checks on his buds daily.
Are they okay? They are okay. They do not need
him, but he speaks, and they listen or at least
shake a leaf. What a world where you can live off
land by loving it. If only we cared for each other
this way. The council cares for their investment.
The late greenery, that is, not Lilian, who shares
his ride on the side. I wonder what it would cost
to have men be tender to me regularly,
to be folded into his burly, to be left on the side
of the road as he drove away, exhausted. Even
my dreams of tenderness involve being used
& I'm not sure who to blame: colonialism,
capitalism, patriarchy, queerness or poetry?
Sorry, this is a commercial for the Kia Sportage
now. This is a commercial for Lilian's thighs.
He has taken me all the way back, around
the future flowering, back to where I am not,
to the homes I keep investing in as harms.
I should fill them with trees. Let the boughs
cover the remembered boy, cowering

under a mother, let life replace memory. Lilian, I left
you that day, and in the leaving, a love
followed. Isn't that a wonder and a wound?
Tell me which it is, I confess I mistake the two.
I walk up the stairs to my old brick apartment
where the peach tree reaches for the railing,
a few blushing fruits poking through the bars,
eager to brush my leg, to say linger, halt.
I want to stop, to hold it for real, just once
but I must wait until I am safe.

OMAR SAKR

End of Text 4

INSIGHT PUBLICATIONS PRACTICE HIGHER SCHOOL CERTIFICATE EXAMINATION

English Standard/Advanced

Paper 1 – Texts and Human Experiences

General Instructions	• Reading time – 10 minutes • Working time – 1 hour and 30 minutes • Write using black pen • A Stimulus Booklet is provided
Total marks: 40	**Section I – 20 marks** • Attempt Questions 1–5 • Allow about 45 minutes for this section **Section II – 20 marks** • Attempt ONE question • Allow about 45 minutes for this section

Note:

This practice examination only contains questions for Section I above.

Section I

20 marks
Attempt Questions 1–5
Allow about 45 minutes for this section

Read the texts on page 160 of the Stimulus Booklet carefully and then answer the questions in the spaces provided. These spaces provide guidance for the expected length of response.

Your answers will be assessed on how well you:

- demonstrate understanding of human experiences in texts
- analyse, explain and assess the ways human experiences are represented in texts.

Question 1 (5 marks)
Text 1 — Prose fiction extract
Analyse how Stevenson has utilised language to capture the narrator's realisation 'that man is not truly one, but truly two.'

If you need additional space to answer Question 1 use the lines below.

Question 2 (3 marks)
Text 2 — Visual text
Analyse how the image celebrates capturing beauty.

If you need additional space to answer Question 2 use the lines below.

Question 3 (4 marks)
Text 3 — Feature article extract

Explain how the author invites the reader to reflect personally on televised experiences of grief and death.

If you need additional space to answer Question 3 use the lines below.

Question 4 (3 marks)
Text 4 — Poem

Analyse how Sakr captures the immigrant experience.

If you need additional space to answer Question 4 use the lines below.

Question 5 (5 marks)
Text 1 and Text 2 OR Text 3 OR Text 4

Compare how Text 1 and ONE other text from the Stimulus Booklet represent duality within the human experience.

If you need additional space to answer Question 5 use the lines below.

INSIGHT PUBLICATIONS PRACTICE HIGHER SCHOOL CERTIFICATE EXAMINATION

English Standard/Advanced

Paper 1 – Texts and Human Experiences

Stimulus Booklet

Notes:

1. This practice examination can be completed by students of both English Standard and English Advanced. In the Higher School Certificate examination, there will be two different papers: you will complete either the Standard paper or the Advanced paper.

2. You will receive two separate booklets for the examination. One is the Stimulus Booklet containing all the unseen texts, and the other is the booklet containing all the questions, where you will write your answers for Section I.

Text 1 — Photograph and graphic

End of Text 1

Text 2 — Poem

Up the Country

I am back from up the country – very sorry that I went –
Seeking for the Southern poets' land whereon to pitch my tent;
I have lost a lot of idols, which were broken on the track,
Burnt a lot of fancy verses, and I'm glad that I am back.
Further out may be the pleasant scenes of which our poets boast,
But I think the country's rather more inviting round the coast.
Anyway, I'll stay at present at a boarding-house in town,
Drinking beer and lemon-squashes, taking baths and cooling down.

'Sunny plains'! Great Scott! – those burning wastes of barren soil and sand
With their everlasting fences stretching out across the land!
Desolation where the crow is! Desert where the eagle flies,
Paddocks where the luny bullock starts and stares with reddened eyes;
Where, in clouds of dust enveloped, roasted bullock-drivers creep
Slowly past the sun-dried shepherd dragged behind his crawling sheep.
Stunted peak of granite gleaming, glaring like a molten mass
Turned from some infernal furnace on a plain devoid of grass.

Miles and miles of thirsty gutters – strings of muddy water-holes
In the place of 'shining rivers' – 'walled by cliffs and forest boles.'
Barren ridges, gullies, ridges! where the ever-madd'ning flies –
Fiercer than the plagues of Egypt – swarm about your blighted eyes!
Bush! where there is no horizon! where the buried bushman sees
Nothing – Nothing! but the sameness of the ragged, stunted trees!
Lonely hut where drought's eternal, suffocating atmosphere
Where the God-forgotten hatter dreams of city life and beer.

Treacherous tracks that trap the stranger, endless roads that gleam and glare,
Dark and evil-looking gullies, hiding secrets here and there!
Dull dumb flats and stony rises, where the toiling bullocks bake,
And the sinister 'gohanna', and the lizard, and the snake.
Land of day and night – no morning freshness, and no afternoon,
When the great white sun in rising bringeth summer heat in June.
Dismal country for the exile, when the shades begin to fall
From the sad heart-breaking sunset, to the new-chum worst of all.
Dreary land in rainy weather, with the endless clouds that drift
O'er the bushman like a blanket that the Lord will never lift –
Dismal land when it is raining – growl of floods, and, oh! the woosh
Of the rain and wind together on the dark bed of the bush –
Ghastly fires in lonely humpies where the granite rocks are piled
In the rain-swept wildernesses that are wildest of the wild.

Land where gaunt and haggard women live alone and work like men,
Till their husbands, gone a-droving, will return to them again:
Homes of men! if home had ever such a God-forgotten place,
Where the wild selector's children fly before a stranger's face.
Home of tragedy applauded by the dingoes' dismal yell,
Heaven of the shanty-keeper – fitting fiend for such a hell –
And the wallaroos and wombats, and, of course, the curlew's call –
And the lone sundowner tramping ever onward through it all!

I am back from up the country, up the country where I went
Seeking for the Southern poets' land whereon to pitch my tent;
I have shattered many idols out along the dusty track,
Burnt a lot of fancy verses – and I'm glad that I am back.
I believe the Southern poets' dream will not be realised
Till the plains are irrigated and the land is humanised.
I intend to stay at present, as I said before, in town
Drinking beer and lemon-squashes, taking baths and cooling down.

HENRY LAWSON

End of Text 2

Text 3 — Online article extract

JOY HESTER – A BODY OF WORK, REMEMBERED AT LAST

I have been thinking a lot lately of how many worlds there are contained in very small spaces and how every person is really one world to himself unconnected by anyone or any thing.

– Joy Hester, 1947

Joy Hester at Fitzroy Gardens, 1942

So said artist Joy Hester, in words that were no doubt a response to dramatic life events that have overshadowed attempts at a sustained critical appreciation of her art.

In 1947, Hester famously left her husband and young son, Sweeney (who was later adopted by Sunday and John Reed) for artist and poet Gray Smith. She was also diagnosed with advanced Hodgkin's Disease which was at that stage an incurable cancer.

Yet, her statement is striking for the fact that Hester's entire body of work, her modus operandi, can be understood as an exploration of human relationships, connections, in all their complexity. A major survey exhibition at Heide now acknowledges this.

Defiant from the start

Born in 1920 to middle-class parents in Melbourne, Hester defied convention from the outset and found a creative and intellectual home in her association with the Victorians Arts Society and at the Contemporary Arts Society in 1938. She joined a group of artists such as Arthur Boyd, Sidney Nolan, John Percival, Danila Vassilieff and Albert Tucker, whom she married in 1941.

She also met the Reeds, patrons of the arts who opened their home 'Heide' to their artistic circle. The couple would become her lifelong supporters, friends and benefactors.

Joy Hester, John Reed with binoculars, Sunday Reed and Sidney Nolan holding Sweeney at the beach in 1945. Albert Tucker/State Library of Victoria

Like most Australian artists of the 1940s and 1950s, Hester's work was a reflection of the huge shifts in Australian culture as it emerged from the violence of war into a definite crisis of national identity.

...

The simplicity of her mark-making in her predominantly pen and ink drawings, appears to be at odds with the often unflinching rawness of the images, leaving the viewer with a sense of uneasiness as to what they are actually witnessing in the work.

Rather than being autobiographical, the characters in her drawings are often amorphous, unidentifiable as her short career (a span of only 20 years) progresses. Hester sought to capture a moment in time that could be easily 'felt' by the viewer.

The female body

The fact Hester's work was focused on the topography of emotions, as well as female bodily experience, no doubt added to its lukewarm reception from male critics in her lifetime.

As Heide senior curator Kendrah Morgan points out in the exhibition catalogue, she was one of the very few Australian women artists to

> *explore female sexuality and do so in a way that neither celebrates the female nude nor eroticism per se, but rather interrogates the sensory and emotional conditions of deep connection and physical intimacy.*

...

The series *Faces* (1947–1948). was described by critic Barrett Reid in 1966 as revealing aspects of human identity at its 'most masked and vulnerable, most exposed, when totally given to powerful emotion'.

Face (With Yellow Background), Joy Hester, circa 1947. Heide Museum of Modern Art/Barrett Reid

Hester herself was disturbed by their intensity as she surveyed them on her wall referring to them as 'frightening things' and almost immediately taking them down.

Searching for self

In the *Love* series (1947–49) we see the artist exploring the complexity of sexual relationships in terms of connection and separateness.

Much of Hester's work concerns itself with the search for identity. This is unsurprising given the expectation of women at the time was in the roles of homemaker and mother.

Untitled (from the Love Series), Joy Hester, 1949. Heide Museum of Modern Art

The interconnectedness of being with another is presented in this series in the shared eyes or mouths or the blurred boundaries between heads. By the time Hester came to *The Lovers* series (1955–56) the blurred boundaries between couples has been replaced with a sense of separateness. The heightened emotions of the female figure are foregrounded and they seem to encompass both despair and euphoria.

Words and pictures

A sense of intimacy is never far away from Hester's unidealised images of children and maternity which appear throughout her work.

...

The Heide retrospective of Hester's work marks the centenary of her birth. It comes at a time when audiences have a much greater sensitivity to her important place in the canon of Australian modernism and as a deeply nuanced artist of the human condition.

The show groups the work together in ways that underline and highlight their emotional impact and provide an important opportunity to connect with the artist and her stunning imagination.

VICTORIA CARRUTHERS
Extract from 'Joy Hester – a body of work, remembered at last'
The Conversation
theconversation.com/joy-hester-a-body-of-work-remembered-at-last-141449

End of Text 3

Text 4 — Feature article extract

WHAT DO WHITE STAFF DO IN REMOTE INDIGENOUS ART CENTRES?

In April, *The Australian* published the results of a four-month investigation into white staff 'interference' at Tjala Arts, a member of the APY Arts Centre Collective of Indigenous art centres across South Australia.

It included a video of an art centre manager painting on Yaritji Young's canvas, to 'juice it up' a bit.

The ongoing media commentary has been divisive and confusing. One question it raises is what do art managers and studio assistants actually do in remote Indigenous community art centres?

50 years of arts centres

Remote art centres are central to today's internationally successful Indigenous contemporary art industry. They typically have a white art centre manager and other staff overseen by an Indigenous board.

Papunya Tula Artists in Central Australia, incorporated in 1972, is the common ancestor of the publicly funded art centre model.

Papunya Tula marked the transition from the paternalism of the mission era to Indigenous self-determination, supported by the establishment of the Aboriginal Arts Board.

On May 3 1973, a press release from Prime Minister Gough Whitlam's office announced:

> *Aboriginals have been given full responsibility for developing their own programs in the arts under a new Government policy to revitalise cultural activities through the Australian Council for the Arts.*

What followed was a revolution, led by and for Aboriginal artists, with non-Indigenous staff employed to mediate with the art world.

Today, this workforce are mostly young women with degrees in visual art or arts management. They operate in around 90 Aboriginal-owned collectives across remote Australia. Staff turnover is high, and recruitment is a perennial task.

A cross-cultural thing

The troubling fact is not that 'Aboriginal art is a white thing', as Aboriginal artist and activist Richard Bell famously declared in 2002. Rather, Aboriginal art is 'a cross-cultural thing', bringing Indigenous and non-Indigenous creative workers together.

Despite the shared goal and triumphs of the cultural industries in celebrating Indigenous art, the shadow of Australia's colonisation is never far away.

The conditions in remote art centres have evolved since the 1970s, but the practicalities are essentially the same. Art centre staff support the artists socially, culturally and logistically to ensure artists are happy to create their work in a culturally safe space.

Staff also manage the external demands of the market, exhibition schedules, bureaucratic accountability (to funding bodies and institutions, for example) and *advocacy*.

...

A collaborative space?

The APY Art Centre Collective management strongly denied allegations of any interference with the paintings or 'the Tjukurrpa' (the Anangu term for their comprehensive spiritual belief system). Their website currently states hands-on assistance, such as 'underpainting', is common practice.

Selecting colours and mixing paint, priming and delegating canvases, washing brushes and general maintenance, as well as regular discussion and responsiveness to the art are all part of the studio assistant's role.

Some aesthetic influence on the final product is only natural, but painting directly on the canvas is never part of the job description. Undeclared, many would consider it fraudulent.

In 1997, when I first went to work in a Western Desert art centre, the message from the artists was simple: sell our paintings, and be straight with us.

It was also clear the paintings offered for sale – to public institutions, knowledgeable collectors and souvenir buyers – would be of a certain standard.

...

In 1996 Kathleen Petyarre won the lucrative Telstra Art Award for her painting Storm in Atnangkere Country II. It was later revealed she was 'assisted' by her white partner.

Following an inquiry, Petyarre retained her rightful authorship of the work, but this prompted art centres to recognise 'creative labour', when delegated by the artist and particularly among family, as culturally accepted practice — which should be attributed accordingly.

The right to determine who gets to collaborate on artwork, and how, applies to artists worldwide. The studios of Jeff Koons and Damien Hirst are extreme examples of art making being undertaken by studio assistants. So too, Aboriginal artists enjoy workshops with specialists in fields as varied as printmaking, bronze casting, animation or glassmaking.

It's up to the artists first, and the institutions, curators, the market and art critics next, to evaluate such collaborations and exchanges case by case.

Cultural narratives and daily realities

A key role in art centres is 'taking the story'. This is where art centre staff document the artist's painting with a photo and the related Tjukurrpa or Country.

These 'certificates of authenticity' documenting culturally important stories guarantee the works as genuine Aboriginal or Torres Strait Islander works. They also underpin the marketing, promotion and interpretation of many contemporary art exhibitions from remote communities.

It's the disconnect between these purist cultural narratives and the realities of the busy cross-cultural studios that puts the artists, their staff and the entire industry in such a paradoxical position.

Trust and ethics lie at the heart of these working relationships. It's impractical to create more rules and impossible to enforce the ways artists and staff interact in art centre settings, but it's time to acknowledge these exchanges with a new story.

UNA REY
Extract from 'What do white staff do in remote Indigenous art centres?'
The Conversation
theconversation.com/what-do-white-staff-do-in-remote-indigenous-art-centres-204746

End of Text 4

INSIGHT PUBLICATIONS PRACTICE HIGHER SCHOOL CERTIFICATE EXAMINATION

English Standard/Advanced

Paper 1 – Texts and Human Experiences

General Instructions

- Reading time – 10 minutes
- Working time – 1 hour and 30 minutes
- Write using black pen
- A Stimulus Booklet is provided

Total marks: 40

Section I – 20 marks

- Attempt Questions 1–4
- Allow about 45 minutes for this section

Section II – 20 marks

- Attempt ONE question
- Allow about 45 minutes for this section

Note:

This practice examination only contains questions for Section I above.

Section I

20 marks
Attempt Questions 1–4
Allow about 45 minutes for this section

Read the texts on page 178 of the Stimulus Booklet carefully and then answer the questions in the spaces provided. These spaces provide guidance for the expected length of response.

Your answers will be assessed on how well you:

- demonstrate understanding of human experiences in texts
- analyse, explain and assess the ways human experiences are represented in texts

---

Question 1 (4 marks)
Text 1 — Photograph and graphic
Compare how the photograph and graphic represent the effect of art on the human experience.

If you need additional space to answer Question 1 use the lines below.

Question 2 (4 marks)

Text 2 — Poem

Explain how the landscape can affect people living 'up the country'.

If you need additional space to answer Question 2 use the lines below.

Question 3 (5 marks)

Text 3 — Online article extract

Explain how the author captures the importance of remembering experiences through art.

If you need additional space to answer Question 3 use the lines below.

Question 4 (7 marks)
Text 4 and Text 1 OR Text 2 OR Text 3

With close reference to Text 4 and ONE other text from the Stimulus Booklet, explain how culture can be both inclusive and divisive.

If you need additional space to answer Question 4 use the lines below.

Useful words to use in your responses

links, ties, connected to, binds, associates, affiliated with, joins

focuses, examines, scrutinises, directed, guides, focalises, centres on, steers toward, specifically

tries to, endeavours to, attempts to, tenuously links to, strives to, undertakes

exploits, uses, takes advantage of, utilises, employs, capitalises on

although, but, however, rather, alternatively, whereas, by contrast, nevertheless, on the other hand, yet, instead, differs from, on the contrary

for example, as shown by, brings to attention, for instance, including, these include, such as

in addition, also, as well as, not only, similarly, furthermore, moreover, besides, likewise, nevertheless

central, crucial, key, necessary, essential, unique, indispensable, primary, major, critical, important, prominent, significant, vital, serious, underlying

CAUSE AND EFFECT	OTHER USEFUL VERBS	EVALUATION
because	accentuates	vitally important
due to	alludes	influences dramatically
as a result of	contradicts	clearly reflects
results in	contests	has serious implications for …
contributes to	contrasts	it is clear that … because …
gives rise to	construes	it is evident that … because …
this influences	correlates	the consequences of this are …
points towards	demonstrates	substantially
brings about	denotes	considerable influence/impact/ role
leads to	evokes	dramatic effect
therefore	exemplifies	to a lesser degree
furthermore	exhibits	to a greater degree
allows for	foreshadows	essential to
consequently	magnifies	fundamental to
it is clear that	negates	a crucial factor
clearly then	signifies	most notably
this could be due to	suggests	relatively
provides insight into	utilises	undeniably
brought about by	enables	this consolidates …
caused by	provokes	it is evident that …
produced by	culminates	it is imperative
stems from	encourages	it is questionable
culminated in	initiates	was arguably
due to	conveys	has a substantial effect upon …
gives rise to	implies	underpins
hence	shapes	
thus	triggers	
	catalyses	
	emphasises	

Acknowledgements

Insight Publications thanks the author, Amanda Lee, for all her work on *Analysing Unseen Texts: For English Standard & English Advanced.* Special thanks to Angela Turco for her advice and review.

Insight Publications is also grateful to the following individuals and organisations for permission to reproduce copyright material.

Texts: NESA website: past exam Question: 'HSC Exam Paper English Advanced Paper 1 - Texts and Human Experiences' and 'HSC Exam Paper English Standard Paper 1 - Texts and Human Experiences' © NSW Education Standards Authority for and on behalf of the Crown in right of the State of New South Wales, 2022; *The Great Gatsby* by F Scott Fitzgerald, Charles Scribner's Sons; *The War of the Worlds* by HG Wells, Pearson's Magazine; 'The Old Things' by Jessie Anderson Chase, Doubleday; *My Brilliant Career* by Miles Franklin, William Blackwood & Sons; '2BR02B' by Kurt Vonnegut, Penguin; 'How the Camel got his Hump' by Rudyard Kipling, Macmillan Publishers; 'Fatal Attraction: young Australians travelling on the edge' by David Beirman, University of Technology Sydney, *The Conversation*; *An Enquiry Concerning Human Understanding* by David Hume, Simon & Schuster; 'Gabrielle Carey was best known for *Puberty Blues* – but I knew her as a formidable intellectual who mastered the art of living well' by Russell Smith, Australian National University, *The Conversation*; 'How *Alone Australia* can help us understand and appreciate our place in nature' by Lily van Eeden, Monash University, Christina Renowden, Monash University, Fern Hames, Arthur Rylah Institute for Environmental Research, Kate Lee, Arthur Rylah Institute for Environmental Research, Melissa Hatty, Monash University, and Sarah Bekessy, RMIT University, *The Conversation*; 'Humanity's tipping point? How the Queen's death stole a climate warning's thunder' by Darren Ray, University of Adelaide, *The Conversation;* 'André Dao's brilliant debut novel explores his grandfather's ten-year detention without trial by the Vietnamese government' by Tess Do, University of Melbourne, *The Conversation;* 'Where They Lived' by Thomas Hardy, Macmillan Publishers; 'As Good as New' by Henry Lawson, Angus and Robertson; 'The Road That Has No End' by Joseph Burrows, Angus and Robertson; 'The Walkers' by Robert William Service, T. Fisher Unwin; 'Landscape' by Charles Baudelaire, Poetry in Translation; 'Ambition and Art' by Banjo Paterson, *The Bulletin*; 'Bram Stoker's Dracula: bats, garlic, disturbing sexualities and a declining empire' by Sharon Bickle, University of Southern Queensland, *The Conversation*; 'Graphic novels help teens learn about racism, climate change and social justice – here's a reading list' by Karen W Gavigan, University of South Carolina, and Kasey Garrison, Charles Sturt University, *The Conversation*; 'Enraged, tragic and hopeful: Alexis Wright's new novel *Praiseworthy* explores Aboriginal sovereignty in the shadow of the Anthropocene' by Jane Gleeson-White, UNSW Canberra, UNSW Sydney, *The Conversation*; 'Peace may finally be returning to Yemen, but can a fractured nation be put back together?' by Leena Adel, Curtin University, and Ben Rich, Curtin University, *The Conversation*; 'Master your anger – or at least try to understand it' by Nick Haslam, The University of Melbourne, *The Conversation;* 'Does Australia "get" culture?' by Julian Meyrick, Flinders University, *The Conversation*; *Strange Case of Dr Jekyll and Mr Hyde* by Robert Louis Stevenson, Longmans, Green & Co.; 'Can death on the screen feel the same as a "real" one?' by Sarah Wayland, University of New England, *The Conversation;* 'Where I Am Not' by Omar Sakr, Academy of American Poets; 'Up the Country' by Henry Lawson, *The Bulletin*; 'Joy Hester – a body of work, remembered at last' by Victoria Carruthers, Australian Catholic University, *The Conversation;* 'What do white staff do in remote Indigenous art centres?' by Una Rey, RMIT University, *The Conversation.*

Images: *They Called Us Enemy*, Penguin Random House, CC BY-SA; Excerpted from "Raw Power" by JF Frankel, in *Wild Ocean: Sharks, Whales, Rays, and Other Endangered Sea Creatures* edited by Matt Dembicki, copyright © 2014 by Matt Dembicki. Used by permission of Chicago Review Press. All rights reserved.; Cover Alexis Wright *Praiseworthy*, Giramondo rights; Cover Alexis Wright *Tracker*, Giramondo rights; Alexis Wright portrait, Vincent Long; Cover Alexis Wright *The Swan Book*, Giramondo rights; Portrait of artist Lena Nyadbi, Alan Porritt/AAP; Joy Hester at Fitzroy Gardens, 1942 (sepia), Albert Tucker/State Library of Victoria; Joy Hester, John Reed with binoculars, Sunday Reed and Sidney Nolan holding Sweeney at the beach in 1945, Albert Tucker/State Library of Victoria; Face (With Yellow Background), 1947 © Joy Hester/Copyright Agency, 2023; Untitled (from the *Love* Series), Joy Hester, 1949 © Joy Hester/Copyright Agency, 2023. The following images from Alamy: Claes Bang in 2020 *Dracula*; Gary Oldman and Winona Ryder in 1992 *Dracula*; Houthi prisoners arriving at airport; Aftermath of car bomb in Yemen, security guard standing watch; Crown Prince Mohammed bin Salman meeting with US president; 50c Stamp – Mrs Edna Everage; Degraves Street Melbourne; *Succession*; *Buffy the Vampire Slayer* still. Additional images from Shutterstock.

Notes: